Moment of Christ

MOMENT OF CHRIST

The Path of Meditation

JOHN MAIN

Crossroad · New York

1984
The Crossroad Publishing Company
370 Lexington Avenue, New York, N.Y. 10017

Printed in the United States of America

Library of Congress Cataloging in Publication Data
Main, John, O.S.B.
  Moment of Christ.
  1. Meditation. 2. Spiritual life—Catholic authors.
I. Title.
BV4813.M313   1984   242   84-12656
ISBN 0-8245-0679-0
ISBN 0-8245-0660-X (pbk.)

Contents

Preface

Perhaps because it was the last thing he wrote, not many weeks before his death, I have re-read Fr John's foreword to this book many times. Although we did not fully understand how close to death he was, it seems to me that he knew it would be his last written message and so he compressed into a few hundred words an experience of prayer and a zeal to lead others into it which, to me, is the essence of wisdom's grand simplicity.

Over my years of discipleship with him I had learned to understand both his own simplicity and the simplicity of his teaching. When he spoke to the groups who came to meditate with us at the monasteries in London and Montreal, groups composed of widely differing types of people, the authority of his simplicity together with his considerable genius for language, anecdote and humour kept the group in profound attention and prepared them, as he intended, not for speculation but for silence.

During the last few years we recorded these talks at each session and then published them as cassettes in our 'Communitas' series. These will continue to be published and to nourish and inspire individuals and groups around the world for some years to come. So it is important to understand the context in which these written words were spoken. The groups met (and still do) at eight o'clock in the evening. One of the community meets newcomers to the Monday night introductory group and shows them down to the meditation-lecture room where people assemble and where music is playing. A few minutes before eight o'clock Fr John enters and sits on a chair near the stereo. He is facing anywhere between forty and a hundred people, some sitting on cushions on the floor, others on chairs lining the walls. The people come from all walks of life, ages and backgrounds. The clock chimes upstairs and, shortly after, Fr John gets up to remove the record. He sits again and sometimes has to be reminded to attach the small microphone to the front of his habit. He quietly clears his throat and begins the talk. There is always a quotation from the New Testament, sometimes opening, sometimes closing the talk. He plays some more quiet music, often Bach or plain-chant, closes it after a few moments ('so that we can leave behind all the words I have been using and enter into the silence of the one word') and resumes his seat for half an hour of meditation. After that he plays some more music and invites questions. Sometimes there are many, sometimes none. In either case he smiles, says a word of farewell and leaves the room, usually to be caught and questioned by people in the hall.

The atmosphere of these groups, with a sizable proportion of people coming straight from work, is extraordinary, silent and attentive and deeply serious. But there is no solemnity, no gimmicks, no rituals, because of the simplicity of what is being taught.

It is important to understand what these talks were designed to do and what Fr John hoped they could still do, even in print. Their aim is to persuade people of the importance and simplicity of the Christian tradition and practice of meditation. They are not therefore theological or philosophical statements. This kind of exposition of the teaching is to be found in his other books such as *Word into Silence*[1] and *Letters from the Heart*[2]. These talks are not designed to stimulate discussion but to inspire a desire for silence and personal discipline.

They are communicating ideas, of course, but also much more than ideas. As everyone who heard these talks in person could testify, they communicated an energy and extraordinary spirit. To be in that room was to know you were in the presence of a man who knew the Presence, was filled with it, joyfully, humorously and profoundly, and who embodied it. It is not very useful to try to describe this, of course. It always struck me how much of this spirit he conveyed by setting people free,

1. Darton, Longman and Todd, 1980.
2. Crossroad, New York, 1982.

not only to be silent but, afterwards, to laugh. It is important to know something of this special presence, if these talks are going to be read in the spirit they were heard in.

Fr John edited most of them, and I the rest. We left in a certain colloquial flavour and quite a lot of repetition. I would advise you not to skip the sentences where you see repetition. Rather I would advise you to read them twice. They are saying the same thing, but if you listen to them you will hear it differently and more deeply each time. I listened to the basic teaching many hundreds or perhaps some thousands of times. It never struck me as monotonous, because each time it was brilliantly set off in a new context, a new facet of the 'many-faceted diamond of God'.

A woman once told me of her experience of coming back to the groups after a year in the north of Canada. She had continued to meditate faithfully through the solitude and difficulty of the year. When she returned to Montreal she suddenly realized to her surprise how frightened she was to come back to the group. What, she thought, if I have been doing this meditation for the last year and now go to hear the talk and find a new teaching and find the old one discarded. Nevertheless, she came and was not betrayed. She could not describe her joy at hearing repeated the same teaching she had committed herself to. And yet she said, it sounded brand new and it was as if she were hearing it for the first time.

A teacher, a true master of the spiritual life like Fr John (who would have smiled at such a solemn title), teaches by gaining the attention of the whole person, not just by addressing the mind with ideas or the feelings with emotions. To be taught like this is itself an experience of the spiritual reality, although like all such experiences it can sound incredibly uninspiring when we come to describe it. I feel these talks in print can lead the reader into the same or a qualitatively similar experience of being in the presence of a great teacher who was filled with the wisdom love gives. If, I suppose, the reader is prepared not only to read but to listen as well.

Benedictine Priory,   LAURENCE FREEMAN, OSB
Montreal.

Foreword

Our purpose in publishing these Communitas talks is to make available the teaching that we give to the groups who come to our monastery on Monday and Tuesday evenings each week.

The essential content of each talk is very simple and is meant to serve as an encouragement to those who are following the path of meditation and to help them to follow that path with greater fervour.

It will be seen that meditation affects every part of our living and dying, and we have tried to include a wide cross-section of the talks that we give.

The usefulness of publishing the talks is that the book can serve as a source for spiritual reading by allowing the reader to turn to any of the talks according to the subject matter. The text is not a continuous narrative but can be entered into at any point.

Perhaps it might be useful to say a general word of introduction to our way of meditating.

It is our conviction that the central message of the New Testament is that there is really only one prayer and that this prayer is the prayer of Christ. It is a prayer that continues in our hearts day and night. I can describe it only as the stream of love that flows constantly between Jesus and his Father. This stream of love is the Holy Spirit.

Again it is our conviction that it is the most important task for any fully human life that we should become as open as possible to this stream of love. We have to allow this prayer to become our prayer, we have to enter into the experience of being swept out of ourselves – beyond ourselves into this wonderful prayer of Jesus – this great cosmic river of love.

In order for us to do this we must learn a way that is a way of silence – of stillness, and this by a discipline that is most demanding. It is as though we have to create a space within ourselves that will allow this higher consciousness – the consciousness of the prayer of Jesus – to envelop us in this powerful mystery.

We have got used to thinking of prayer in terms of 'my prayer' or 'my praise' of God, and it requires a complete rethinking of our attitude to prayer if we are going to come to see it as a way through Jesus, with Jesus, and in Jesus.

The first requirement is that we begin to understand that we must pass beyond egoism, so that 'my' prayer just doesn't become even a possibility. We are summoned to see with the eyes of Christ and to love with the heart of Christ, and to respond to this summons we must pass beyond egoism. In practical terms this means learning to be so still and silent that we cease thinking about ourselves. This is of critical importance – we must be open to the Father through Jesus, and when we are at prayer we must become like the eye that can see but that cannot see itself.

The way we set out on this pilgrimage of 'other-centredness' is to recite a short phrase, a word that is commonly called today a mantra. The mantra is simply a means of turning our attention beyond ourselves – a way of unhooking us from our own thoughts and concerns.

Reciting the mantra brings us to stillness and to peace. We recite it for as long as we need to before we are caught up into the one prayer of Jesus. The general rule is that we must first learn to say it for the entire period of our meditation each morning and each evening and then to allow it to do its work of calming over a period of years.

The day will come when the mantra ceases to sound and we are lost in the eternal silence of God. The rule when this happens is not to try to possess this silence, to use it for one's own satisfaction. The clear rule is that as soon as we consciously realize that we are in this state of profound silence and begin to reflect about it we must gently and quietly return to our mantra.

Gradually the silences become longer and we are simply absorbed in the mystery of God. The important thing is to have the courage and generosity to return to the mantra as soon as we become self-conscious of the silence.

It is important not to try to invent or anticipate any of the experiences. I hope that, reading these talks, it will become clear that each of us is summoned to the heights of Christian prayer – each of us is summoned to fullness of life. What we need however is the humility to tread the way very faithfully over a period of years so that the prayer of Christ may indeed be the grounding experience of our life.

Montreal,
October 1982

JOHN MAIN, OSB

The Way of the Mantra

The most important part of our time together in our groups is that time we spend being silent together. Silence is the best preparation for meditation. When you begin to meditate, spend a couple of moments getting really comfortable. If you want to sit in a chair, sit in an upright one. If you sit on the floor, sit in a comfortable position. Then try to be as still as you can for the entire time of the meditation. It isn't all that easy for most of us when we start, but meditation involves coming to a stillness of spirit and a stillness of body. It gives you an awareness of yourself as one, as still, as whole. So you have to learn to sit as still as you can. When you are seated and are still, close your eyes and then begin to repeat, interiorly and silently in your heart, the word *Maranatha*. In some traditions, this is called a 'mantra', in others, a 'prayer phrase' or 'prayer word'.

The essence of meditation and the art of meditation is simply learning to say that word, to recite it, to sound it, from the beginning to the end of the meditation. It is utterly simple – say it like this: 'Ma-ra-na-tha'. Four equally stressed syllables. Most people say the word in conjunction with their breathing, but that isn't of the essence. The essence requires that you say the word from beginning to end and continue to say it right throughout your meditation time. The speed should be something that is fairly slow, fairly rhythmical – 'Ma-ra-na-tha'. And that is all you need to know in order to meditate. You have a word, and you say your word, and you remain still.

The purpose of meditation for each of us is that we come to our own centre. In many traditions, meditation is spoken of as a pilgrimage – a pilgrimage to your own centre, your own heart, and there you learn to remain awake, alive and still. The word 'religion' means a 're-linking', being 'rebound' to your own centre. The importance of meditation is to discover from your own experience that there is only one centre and that the life task for all of us is to find our source and our meaning by discovering and living out of that one centre.

I think that what we have to understand is that returning to our centre, discovering our own centre, is the first task and the first responsibility of every life that is to become fully human. Again, in meditation, in the discipline of it, you will discover from your own experience that to be at one with our own centre means that we are at one with every centre.

The truly spiritual man or woman is one who is in harmony, one who has discovered that harmony within themselves and *lives* this harmony with creation and with God. What we learn in meditation is that to be in our own centre is to be in God. This is not only the great teaching of all Eastern religions but it is the fundamental insight of Christianity. In the words of Jesus, 'The kingdom of heaven is within you.' And the kingdom, in the teaching of Jesus, is an experience. It is an experience of the power of God. It is an experience of the basic energy of the universe. And, again in the vision of Jesus, we understand that this basic power, out of which we are invited to live our own lives vitally, is love. The Christian experience is learning to live at this level of reality. St John of the Cross expressed this when he said that he knew that God was the centre of his soul. Each one of us is invited to discover the validity of that statement from our own experience. The invitation is to discover, at the centre, both energy and power, and in silence, in stillness, to discover in that power the peace that is beyond all understanding.

We have to use certain words to talk about this. We use words like 'enlightenment' or 'vitalization'. But they are terms that we use to describe what can only be *known*. And the wonder of the experience of prayer, of deep meditation, is that in the experience of the power of God we awaken to reality – a reality that is everywhere. What we discover is that we cannot know that reality from outside, and this for the very simple reason that there is no reality outside of God. That is why we must enter within. We must leave the world of illusion and enter the world of reality. The energy released in meditation is not an energy that is released and received from some outside force. It is the very life-force that each of us possesses, coming to fulfilment, coming to actualization when we turn our whole attention beyond ourselves to the Other. This is the experience of transcendence. This is the expansion of spirit that brings each of us wholly into the gift of our own being.

What we have to discover in meditation is that we *are*, that we are alive, that we are real and that we are rooted in reality. Talking about prayer or about meditation or talking about God serves only one purpose – not to teach us anything 'new' but to reveal to us what is present, what is actual, what is real. To sit down to meditate, to sit down to be still, we need simplicity. We need to become childlike. We must understand that the peace within us is beyond all understanding. We are invited to enter wholly into the experience of it. Meditation, we might describe, as accepting fully the gift of our own continuous creation.

But above all we must beware of becoming intoxicated by the words. Let me end by repeating for you the process that leads us to simplicity, to silence, to awareness and to transcendence which is leaving ourselves behind, leaving our own thoughts behind, leaving our imagination and our own ideas behind. The way is the way of the mantra, of *the* word. When you sit down, sit still and comfortably, begin to say your word and say it from the beginning to the end – 'Ma-ra-na-tha'.

St Paul wrote this to the Corinthians:

For the same God who said, 'Out of darkness let light shine', has caused his light to shine within us, to give the light of revelation – the revelation of the glory of God in the face of Jesus Christ.[1]

The power of this light is to be found within our own hearts, within each one of us. What each of us must learn to do is to be open to that power and to live our lives out of it. What I

1. 2 Cor. 4:6

3

suggest to you is that you try to build into the structure of your life a time each morning and evening to be still, to be silent, to be humble, to be simple, to be *in* God.

Leaving Distractions Behind

Learning to meditate is the most practical thing in the world. You require only one quality when you begin. That is seriously to want to learn to meditate. The process is absolute simplicity. In general, we are obsessed with the idea of techniques, methods, methodologies, and so on, but in meditation the Way is simplicity itself. Let me describe it to you again.

You need to find a quiet place, as quiet as you can and, having found it, you sit down. I recommend you to close your eyes gently and then to begin to say your word. The word I have suggested that you say is the word *maranatha*. It is an Aramaic word and its importance is both that it is one of the most ancient Christian prayers there is and that it possesses the right sound to bring us to the silence and stillness necessary for meditation. That's all there is. Sit upright, and remain sitting upright. Then in a growing stillness of body and spirit say your word, 'Ma-ra-na-tha'.

I want now to address a particular question that we all encounter. It is the question of distractions. What should you do when you begin to meditate and distracting thoughts come into your mind? The advice that the tradition has to give us is to ignore the distractions and to say your word and to keep on saying your word. Don't waste any energy in trying to furrow your brow and say, 'I will not think of what I'm going to have for dinner', or 'who I'm going to see today', or 'where I'm going tomorrow', or whatever the distraction may be. Don't try to use any energy to dispel the distraction. Simply ignore it and the way to ignore it is to say your word.

In other words, when you meditate your energy must be channelled in a single course, and the way of that course is your word. You can't fully appreciate this advice outside of the experience of meditation. Meditation is, as I have suggested to you, about stillness. It is like the stillness of a pool of water. The distractions that we have when we begin to meditate are only ripples and currents and eddies that disturb the water. But as you begin to meditate, and stillness comes over you, the depth of the water becomes clearer and clearer in the stillness. The experience of meditation, the experience to which each of us is summoned and which all of us are capable of, is to discover that depth within us which is like a deep pool of water, water of an infinite depth. The marvellous thing about such a pool of water is that when it is still and the sun strikes it, every drop of the water in its infinite depth is like a drop of crystal alive with the light of the sun. That is exactly what we are called to in meditation – to discover the depth of our own spirit and the capacity of our own spirit to be in complete harmony with the God who tells us that he is light. 'I am the light of the world.'

Don't misunderstand this. As I have told you with absolute truth, meditation *is* simplicity itself. But you do have to be serious in your own commitment to this deep harmony within your own spirit – a harmony that reveals to you the spirit of God within you. You have to be serious.

Consider the problem of distraction again. One of the things that all of us find as we tread our path of meditation with simplicity and with humility is that there will be certain things in our lives that have to change. For example, I should think it would be very difficult to meditate if you spend three or four hours a day watching television. A great enemy of all prayer and of all recollection is a plethora of images in our minds. You will all discover, and I am sure you are already discovering it from your own experience, that it is foolishness to add indiscriminately to this plethora of images.

Listen to the words of St Paul writing to the Corinthians, 'Remember: sparse sowing, sparse reaping; sow bountifully, and you will reap bountifully.'[1] There is a marvellous harvest for all of us in our own spirit. But the call to this openness to the spirit of Jesus does ask for real generosity from each of us. Firstly we need generosity in putting aside the half-hour for

1. 2 Cor. 9:6

6

meditation every morning and every evening. And I understand very well that that does ask for a very generous response and a very creative response, given the tasks and responsibilities of your own lives. Secondly, a great generosity is called for in the actual time of your meditation to say your word, *maranatha*, from the beginning to the end. So often we want to follow our own thoughts, our own insights, our own religious feeling. But we must learn to leave everything behind and to seek the spirit in our own hearts.

Thirdly, there is the generosity needed to put our whole life into harmony with the spirit in our heart – to see to it that we don't add to the distractions. All of us have distractions arising from our very life. We all have things we are concerned about, things we are worried about, things we are responsible for. So what we must do is put our whole life into harmony with this search, this pilgrimage, which is a pilgrimage to our own heart. It is a pilgrimage that leads us to a freshness of spirit, a clarity of heart and a vitality of spirit. Meditation is not turning our back on our life or on our responsibilities. Quite the contrary, in meditation we seek to be open fully to the gift of the life that is given us. This is nothing less than the gift of eternal life, eternal life that we are invited to be open to *now*. We need to be responsible people, to be *responsive* people, responsive to the gift of eternal life. As Jesus tells us, eternal life is to know our heavenly Father. In meditation we turn aside from everything that is passing away in order to know what is eternal.

Now let me remind you. Sit down when you go to meditate. Sit comfortably with your spine upright. Close your eyes and very peacefully and serenely begin to say your word in your heart – silently – 'Ma-ra-na-tha'. Forget the time. We will meditate for about twenty-five minutes. You have to *be* during that time. To be at peace, to be still, still in body and still in spirit and to be open to life and to the Lord of life.

Listen again to St Paul writing to the Corinthians:

For the love of Christ leaves us no choice, when once we have reached the conclusion that one man died for all and therefore all mankind has died. His purpose in dying for all was that men, while still in life, should cease to live for

7

themselves, and should live for him who for their sake died and was raised to life.[2]

2. 2 Cor. 5:14–15

A Call to Fullness of Life

One of the great difficulties about learning to meditate is that it is so simple. In our society most people think that only very complex things are worthwhile. To meditate you have to learn to be simple, and that provides a real challenge for all of us.

The simplicity that is involved in learning to meditate is turning away from multiplicity and from all the options that are before us and concentrating in utter simplicity of being. Think of learning to ride a bike. To learn how to ride it you have first of all to learn to balance yourself on the bike. And later you have to concentrate both on keeping your balance and steering a straight course. The extraordinary thing is that as you do devote all your energies to being balanced and steady you discover unexpected harmony and a new freedom. The same is true with meditation. Like learning to ride a bike you have to be willing to learn. You have to be willing to concentrate. You have to learn to direct all your energies to the simple task of being balanced and travelling steadily in one direction.

To be *on the way* in meditation you have to be simple enough to turn aside from everything else so that you can really be harmonious and free. Meditation is openness to a reality that we can only discover and only encounter in the depths of our own being. So we have to learn to be silent and to be profoundly silent. The extraordinary thing is that, in spite of all the distractions of the modern world, this silence is perfectly possible for all of us. To descend into this silence we have to devote time, energy and love. The first thing you have to understand about meditating is that you have to devote the time to it. It is necessary to meditate every morning and every evening. The minimum amount of time is twenty minutes. I recommend you, as gently as you can, to extend that to about half an hour.

Now let me just repeat to you what is to be done in that time. Sit down and spend a couple of moments in sitting comfortably so you can stay still in the same position for the whole time. Then close your eyes and begin to recite your mantra interiorly, in silence. The art of meditating is to learn to recite your word from the beginning of your meditation to the end, 'Maranatha'. I cannot over-emphasize to you how important that is. What I would suggest to you is never be deflected from the path of saying your word, your mantra, from the beginning to the end of your meditation time. You should sound it silently in your heart. It's the sounding of the word interiorly that opens up for us levels of awareness that are not possible outside this depth of silence. I said that meditation is a learning process. But most learning processes that we are familiar with are learning processes in which we are learning to do something. Meditation is not learning to do, it is learning to *be*. It's learning to *be yourself*, to enter into the gift of your own being. We have come to understand this very clearly and confidently. Another way of putting the same thing would be to say that meditation is learning to accept the gift of your own being, of your own creation. To be in harmony with your own being and with your own continuous creation is also to be in harmony with all of the creation around us, it is being in harmony with the Creator.

One thing we learn in meditation is the priority of being over action. Indeed, no action has any meaning, or at least any lasting depth of meaning, unless it springs from being, from the depths of your own being. That is why meditation is a way that leads us away from shallowness to depth, to profundity. Learning to be is learning to begin to live out of the fullness of life. That is our invitation. It is learning to begin to be a full person. The mysterious thing about the Christian revelation is that as we live our lives fully, we live out the eternal consequences of our own creation. We are no longer living as if we were exhausting a limited supply of life that we received at our birth. What we know from the teaching of Jesus is that we become infinitely filled with life when we are at one with the source of our being and enter fully into union with our Creator, the One who *is*, a God who describes himself as 'I Am'.

The art of living, living our lives as fully human beings, is the art of living out of the eternal newness of our origin and living fully from our centre, which is to say from our spirit as it springs from the creative hand of God. The terrible thing about so much modern, materialistic living is that it can be so shallow, without a serious recognition of the depths and the possibilities that are there for each of us if only we will take the time and undertake the discipline to meditate. The discipline is to sit down to meditate and during meditation to say our word from the beginning to the end, every morning and every evening.

In the Christian vision we are led to this source of our being by a guide, and our guide is Jesus, the fully realized man, the man wholly open to God. As we meditate each day we may not recognize our guide. That is why the Christian journey is always a journey of faith. But as we approach the centre of our being, as we enter our heart, we find that we are greeted by our guide, greeted by the one who has led us. We are welcomed by the person who calls each one of us into personal fullness of being. The consequences or results of meditation, are just this fullness of life – harmony, oneness and energy, a divine energy that we find in our own heart, in our own spirit. That energy is the energy of all creation. As Jesus tells us, it is the energy that is love.

The vision is a staggering vision and we have to learn, as I am saying, to be simple and humble as we approach it. The simplicity and the humility we learn by saying our word from beginning to end, with patience and with faithfulness, with courage and with love. Listen to the words of St Paul writing to the Philippians:

I count everything sheer loss, because all is far outweighed by the gain of knowing Christ Jesus my Lord, for whose sake I did in fact lose everything. I count it so much garbage, for the sake of gaining Christ and finding myself incorporate in him. . . . All I care for is to know Christ, to experience the power of his resurrection, and to share his sufferings, in

11

growing conformity with his death, if only I may finally arrive at the resurrection from the dead. . . . He will transfigure the body belonging to our humble state, and give it a form like that of his own resplendent body, by the very power which enables him to make all things subject to himself. Therefore, my friends, beloved friends whom I long for, my joy, my crown, stand firm in the Lord.[1]

That is what meditation summons us to – to experience in our own spirit the power of the resurrection with Jesus.

1. Phil. 3:8, 10–11, 21—4:1

Infinite Expansion of Love

These words of Jesus are reported in the Gospel of St John:

> In very truth, anyone who gives heed to what I say and puts his trust in him who sent me has hold of eternal life, and does not come up for judgement, but has already passed from death to life.[1]

Meditation is focused right in the heart, right in the centre of the Christian mystery. And the Christian mystery can only be penetrated if we enter into the mystery of death and resurrection. That is the essential message of Jesus. No one can be a follower of Jesus unless he leaves self behind. The person who would find his life must be ready to lose it.[2] And in all the parables drawn from nature which Jesus gives, the seed must fall into the ground and die, or it remains alone.

What we do in meditation and in the life-long process of meditation is to refine our perception down to the single focal point which is Christ. Christ is our way, our goal, our guide. But he is our goal only in the sense that once we are wholly with him, wholly at one with him, we pass with him to the Father. In meditation we come to that necessary single-pointedness and find it is Christ.

It is impossible to talk about meditation as it is impossible to talk about the Christian experience in any adequate terms. As one philosopher put it, 'As soon as we begin to speak of the mysteries of Christ, we hear the gates of heaven closing.' Yet we have to try to speak, though we speak only to bring people to silence. The silence of our meditation is our way into

1. John 5:24   2. cf. Mark 8:35

the indescribable mystery to be found within the heart of each one of us, if only we will undertake this pilgrimage to one-pointedness, to single-mindedness. We have to find some way of trying to explain what the journey is and why the journey is so worthwhile and why it requires courage.

The modern consciousness is not very keen on the idea of narrowness. Yet meditation is a way by which we focus our attention. We *narrow* our attention down to one point. It seems to me that it might help you to understand what meditation is about if you can see it as a great double triangle.

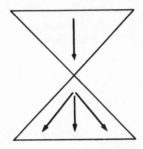

Here you have the triangle on the top, pointing down and then the triangle underneath it, opening out. The triangle on the top is learning to concentrate, learning to focus our attention entirely upon and within Christ. In that sense it is narrowing our attention to a single point. But as soon as we do, the way is opened to infinite expansion on the other side. A single point thus leads us into infinite expansion. It is through Jesus that we pass over from everything that is dead, from everything that is restricted, mortal and finite, into the infinite expansion of God which is infinite expansion of love.

As we come to that one-pointedness we need courage. We need the courage to persevere, not to be afraid of the narrowness and not to be afraid of the demand that is being made on us. The demand *is* an absolute demand, the demand of faith, to believe that what Jesus says is true when he says that if we lose our life, then and only then, will we be able to find it.

Meditation is like breaking through the sound barrier. When you come to that point there can be a lot of turbulence. It is at this moment that the discipline you have learned by saying your mantra and by faithfully continuing to say it, will enable you to be entirely open to the love of Jesus which takes you through it. We need discipline to love and to be open to love because we need discipline to be free. As we approach that point it seems that we require great courage. It seems that we require great perseverance. What we come to know is that all the courage and all the capacity to persevere are freely ours in Jesus.

This is the intoxicating foundation of the whole Christian mystery – that the passover is accomplished. It is achieved in Jesus and it is his courage, his faithfulness and his love that take us into the infinite expansion that is God. So there is no essential ground for our fear, for our postponement, for our holding back. Everything *is* ours in the love of Jesus. Our task is a very humble one. It is the task of acknowledging and entering into our own poverty. We do that by saying our word, by faithful commitment to our mantra. It is a very humble task but it is a task that leads us into the infinite love of God.

We have to remember that the axis of Christian life is death and resurrection. The resurrection is to new life, limitless life, eternal life. Jesus tells us that if we are open to him, if we have the courage to listen to him, to hear what he says, then eternal life, infinite life and the infinite expansion of life is ours. That is the mystery. That is what we are invited to be open to. That is what we are invited to proclaim to the world.

The Way is the way of daily fidelity, a daily aligning and re-aligning of our lives on the mystery that is simplicity, that is love, that is unity. Listen to Jesus again, 'In very truth, anyone who gives heed to what I say and puts his trust in him who sent me has hold of eternal life and does not come up for judgement but has already passed from death to life.'

Discipline and Liberty

One of the things that I suppose everybody strives for in their life is to discover a real liberty of spirit. We are constrained by so many things – by fear and by trying to project the image of ourselves that we feel others expect. I think people suffer a great deal of frustration because they cannot be themselves and cannot make contact with themselves. James Joyce once described one of his characters as 'always living at a certain distance from himself'. Now what Jesus came to proclaim was precisely this liberty. The liberty to be ourselves and the liberty to find ourselves in him, through him and with him. Meditation is simply the way to that liberty. It is the way to your own heart. It is the way to the depth of your own being where you can simply *be* – not having to justify yourself or to apologize for yourself but simply rejoicing in the gift of your own being. Freedom is not just freedom *from* things. Christian liberty is not just freedom from desire, from sin. We are free *for* intimate union with God, which is another way of saying we are free for infinite expansion of Spirit in God.

Meditation is entering into that experience of being free for God, transcending desire, sin, leaving it behind; transcending ego, leaving it behind, so that the whole of our being is utterly available to God. It is in that profound availability that we become ourselves. Consider these words of Jesus:

> Turning to the Jews who had believed in him, Jesus said, 'If you dwell within the revelation I have brought, you are indeed my disciples; you shall know the truth, and the truth will set you free.[1]

1. John 8:31–2

16

Meditation is simply dwelling within the revelation, dwelling within the vision of God.

To meditate each of us must learn to be wholly still and that is a discipline. When you meditate you should spend a few moments just getting into a comfortable sitting posture. But then all of us at some time during our meditation feel like moving and by not moving, by staying still, we will undergo what may perhaps be our first lesson in transcending desires and overcoming that fixation that we so often have with ourselves. So I want you to understand that meditation does involve this real discipline and the first discipline we probably have to learn is to sit quite still. That is why it is important to take care of the practical details like wearing loose clothing, and finding a comfortable chair or cushion to sit on, so that you can be comfortable and so enter in fully and generously to the discipline.

Then you close your eyes gently and begin to repeat your word – 'Maranatha'. The purpose of repeating the word is to gently lead you away from your own thoughts, your own ideas, your own desire, your own sin and to lead you into the presence of God, by turning you around, by turning you away from yourself towards God. Say the word gently but deliberately, say the word in a relaxed way but articulate it silently in your mind, 'Ma-ra-na-tha'. Gradually, as you continue to meditate, the word will sink down into your heart. And this experience of liberty of spirit is the uniting of mind and heart in God.

As you begin to meditate all sorts of questions will arise in your mind. Is this for me? What does it mean? Should I be doing this? Am I getting anything out of it? and so forth. All these questions you must leave behind. You must transcend all self-questioning, and you must come to your meditation with childlike simplicity. Unless you become like little children, you *cannot* enter the Kingdom of Heaven.

So my advice to you is, say your word, be content to say your word and allow the gift to be given by God. Don't demand it. We should come to our meditation with no demands and no expectations, but with just that generosity of spirit that allows us to be as present as we can to ourselves and to God. Meditating is very, very simple. Don't complicate it. As you meditate

17

you should become more and more simple, not more and more complicated. As you know, nothing in this life that is really worth having, can be had without a considerable amount of self-transcendence. It is the real loss of self that brings us the joy. And meditating is having the nerve to take the attention off yourself and to put it forward, to put it forward on God, to look ahead.

We are used to dwelling in a world with thousands of mirrors, seeing ourselves, seeing how others see us, constantly. Meditating is a definitive smashing of all the mirrors. It is looking, not at reflections of things, not at reflections of yourself. It is looking into the reality that is God. And, in that experience, being expanded into infinity. That is liberty of spirit. The liberty is the fruit of the discipline and so if you want to learn to meditate it is absolutely necessary to meditate every day. Every day of your life, every morning and every evening. There are no short-cuts. There are no crash courses. There is no instant mysticism. It is simply the gentle and gradual change of direction. The change of heart that comes is to stop thinking of yourself and to be open to God, to the wonder of him, to the glory of him and to the love of him.

Silent Communion

In our Community we are trying to share, as widely as we can, the tradition of Christian meditation. We hold the conviction in our Community here that all the spiritual riches of the New Testament, the full riches of what Christ came to proclaim, are available for each of us if only we can enter into his experience. Look simply and clearly at the New Testament and you will see that the central thrust of the Gospel is this proclamation of fullness of life, fullness of being. And the fullness of life it speaks of comes from living out of the depths of our being. This conviction of the New Testament grew out of the experience of the men who made the proclamation that all of us are invited to live our lives out of the power of God, the power of his love. To 'enter the kingdom of God' is simply to live our life out of this power and to have our lives transformed by it.

What we have to share, out of the tradition of monastic prayer, is that this power is to be discovered in all of us when we commit ourselves to *depth* of living and when we commit ourselves with all seriousness. The language of the New Testament described this commitment as being 'rooted and founded in Christ'. I think we might describe this in more modern language as the full acceptance by each one of us of the challenge to *be*. The New Testament also used the word 'maturity'. That is what we are called to by this challenge. An adult acceptance of all the challenges and the responsibilities of life leads to 'fullness of being'. What is abundantly clear from reading the New Testament is that the call of Christians is a call to 'growth', to 'depth', and equally clear is that this depth and maturity take place 'in Christ'. Here we enter the heart of the Christian mystery. To 'be a Christian' is to be one with Christ. Putting this another way, it means that to be a Christian

19

is to live your life out of the resources of your union with Christ. This is precisely what Christian prayer is about.

This union of course clarifies our perception. We must be very clear of what it is about or we are in danger of missing the whole point of Christianity. The call of Jesus is to oneness with him, so that with him we may be one with the Father. So what we have to try to remember and be always mindful of is that the essence of Christian prayer is not dialogue but union, oneness. I think most of us know this in our heart of hearts. We know from our own experience that if we see prayer as dialogue, 'dialoguing with God', it frequently ends up as a monologue.

The tradition that we follow as Benedictine monks calls us both to understand and to experience our prayer as silent communion within our own heart. Union brings us to communion, that is to a oneness discovered within ourselves but which leads us to oneness with God and to oneness with all. It is a communion that is indescribably enriching, because it takes us right out of ourselves, beyond ourselves into union with all, with the All, with God. Unity, union, communion is the three-fold growth of a Christian.

The experience of prayer is the experience of coming into full union with the energy that created the universe. What Christianity has to proclaim to the world is that that energy is love and it is the well-spring out of which all creation flows. It is the well-spring that gives each one of us the creative power to be the person we are called to be – a person rooted and founded in love.

Our tradition tells us all that, but it tells us still more. It tells us too that this is not just poetry. Our practice of meditation tells us that this is the *experience* to which each of us is summoned. The way to it is the way of simplicity and of faithfulness. What our tradition teaches is that to enter this mystery we must learn to be silent. Meditation is entry into profound silence. To meditate means to live out of the centre of our being,that profound centre we find when we determine not to be shallow, not to be content to rest on the surface but to live out of the depths of our being. We must opt for this, because it is in the depths of our being that the union with Christ is continuously taking place. The path to follow is a path of almost incredible simplicity and this is perhaps a good part of the difficulty for us as men and women of the twentieth century. To enter into the simplicity of it demands courage. To meditate, each of us must learn to be very simple, to be very quiet, to learn to say our word.

When we meditate the first thing to do, after sitting down, is to spend a couple of moments getting comfortable, knowing that during your meditation you are going to sit as still as you can. Close your eyes. Then you begin to say your word. The word I recommend you to say is the word, *maranatha* (an ancient Christian prayer, in Aramaic, the language of Jesus, which means, 'Come, Lord'). The art of meditation, and what we have to learn, is to say the word from the beginning to the end of our meditation and to say it effortlessly, peacefully, serenely: 'Maranatha', four syllables – ma-ra-na-tha. It is the recitation of the word that gradually, over a period of weeks and months and years, brings you to that depth, to that silence.

Now when you begin, you have to take this on faith. You have to learn to accept it as part of a tradition. To learn to be faithful to it you have to try, as best you can in the circumstances of your own life, to meditate every morning and every evening. As I said, meditation is a commitment to depth and a turning aside from shallow, surface approaches to living and to understanding life. It is certainly my own experience that the minimum that is required if you are serious about learning to meditate, is to take that half-an-hour slot in the morning and again in the evening every day. During your half-hour each morning and each evening follow the same routine. But it is never the same. Choose a quiet place, sit comfortably. The only essential rule of posture is that your spine is upright. You can either sit on the floor on a cushion or on a chair, whichever is more comfortable for you and then, with every muscle in your body relaxed, including the muscles of your face, begin to recite your word, gently, peacefully, serenely but continuously.

If you are patient and if you are faithful (and meditation will teach you to be both patient and faithful), then meditation will bring you into deeper and deeper realms of silence. It is in the silence that we are led into the mystery of the eternal silence of God. This is what St Paul says when writing to the Ephesians and telling the ordinary people of Ephesus, people who are not that different from us – what is the promise of the Christian life:

> So he came and proclaimed the good news; peace to you who were far off and peace to those who were nearby; for through him, we both alike have access to the Father in the one Spirit.[1]

That is what meditation is about – access to the Father in the one Spirit, the Spirit who dwells in your heart and in mine, the Spirit who is the Spirit of God. Christian meditation is simply openness to that Spirit, in the depth of our being, in all simplicity, in all humility, in all love.

1. Eph. 2:17

The Peace of Christ

There is an aspect of meditation that experience makes us all familiar with. It is an aspect that is deeply inserted into the Christian tradition. The Christian knows that Jesus is the Way, the Truth and the Life. And as he himself told us, he came to give us his peace and to leave us peace. St Luke begins his gospel saying that Christ came 'to guide our feet into the way of peace'.[1] Christian peace is something unique and we can only encounter it in Christ.

As St Paul puts it in the Letter to the Romans, 'Let us continue at peace with God through our Lord Jesus Christ'.[2] Meditation is our way into the peace of Christ because he dwells in our heart, and in meditation we seek him in our heart because 'he himself is our peace'.[3] In his letter to the Ephesians Paul speaks of Christ as having broken down all the barriers symbolized by the dividing wall in the Temple, which separated the outer from the inner court, the outer from the inner reality. In Christ reality is one again.

Meditation does just that in our own lives. It breaks down all the barriers set up within us, between our outer and inner life and brings the whole of us into harmony. The peace of Christ, which is beyond all understanding, beyond all analysis, arises from this unity. The choice proposed by Paul, the challenge in Paul, is to live according to the Spirit which creates this unity. In other words we are invited to live out of the fullness of power that is there in the heart of each of us, if only we will turn to it and if only we will be open to it.

What Paul is saying is that the invitation is to live out of the depth of our being, not according to the surface or to 'the flesh'

1. Luke 1:79   2. Rom. 5:1   3. Eph. 2:14

23

or to 'the world'. What Paul sees so clearly is that the world and the flesh divorced from the Spirit can only lead to death. But the Spirit enlivens everything, fills everything with life, including the world and the flesh. It enlivens by calling all into unity with Christ. All things, the whole of creation are brought into unity in Christ. This is the source of our peace.

In the Christian vision of the New Testament peace arises from harmony, communion with God. 'Peace is my gift to you,' said Jesus.[4] In his farewell discourse at the Last Supper, as reported by John, Jesus speaks of his return to the Father, and then he adds, 'I have told you all this so that in me you may find peace.'[5]

Now meditation is our way to peace. A commitment to silence is the first step into finding this peace of Christ. We discover in the practice of meditation, returning to it day after day, morning and evening, that the silence which is the peace of Christ enables us to be fully awake, fully alive. It is a silence of wakefulness and vitality because it is a silence filled with God's presence. Christian prayer is a commitment to a silence in which we find our own roots in the eternal silence of God, a silence in which we enter into profound harmony and find ourselves in communion.

The way of prayer is the way of union, of oneness. No Greek, no Jew, no male, no female – but eternal harmony and eternal fulfilment in God. This was the message of Paul writing to the Ephesians:

> Your world was a world without hope and without God. But now, in union with Christ Jesus, you who once were far off have been brought near through the shedding of Christ's blood. For he is himself our peace. Gentiles and Jews, he has made the two one, and in his own body of flesh and blood he has broken down the enmity which stood like a dividing wall between them; for he annulled the law with its rules and regulations, so as to create out of the two, a single new humanity in himself, thereby making peace.[6]

Meditation is a commitment to unity, and so it involves a

4. John 14:27   5. John 16:33   6. Eph. 2:12–15

turning away from alienation, from external divisions and from internal dividedness. The spiritual man or woman is one who is 'in love' – in love within themselves beyond dividedness, and loving towards all the brethren beyond division. And most miraculously we are in love with God beyond all alienation, in Jesus. St Paul ends that section 'for through him we both alike have access to the Father in the one Spirit'. If you leave it at the level of words Christianity is unbelievable. We couldn't believe that it is our destiny to have such perfect access to the Father and the Spirit. It is beyond what the human mind could think of or comprehend. It is only in the experience of prayer that the truth of the Christian revelation engulfs us. That is the invitation of Christian prayer, to lose ourselves and to be absorbed in God.

Commitment to Simplicity

The more we talk about meditation the more we need to remind ourselves of it as a way of simplicity. Simplicity is the condition of goodness, happiness, blessedness and we learn simplicity through poverty. Jesus taught, 'How blessed [how happy] are those who know that they are poor; the kingdom of heaven is theirs.'[1]

As a goal simplicity is something very unfamiliar to us. Most of us are carefully trained to see that only complexity is really worthy of respect. To understand simplicity we have to enter into it ourselves. We have to enter the simplicity of God and be simplified ourselves in the process.

You have heard it said, I am sure, that meditation is 'the way to reality'. It is firstly the way to the reality of our own being. By meditating, we learn to *be*. Not to be any particular role or particular thing but just to *be*. The best way of describing that being is to say that we are in a state of utter simplicity. We are not trying to act. We are not trying to apologize for being who we are or as we are. We are, simply, living out of the depths of our own being, secure and affirmed in our own rootedness in reality. As I say, this is an ideal unfamiliar to most of us because we are trained to think that we find truth only amid complexity. Yet I think we all know at a deeper level of our being that truth can only be found in utter simplicity, in openness. Remembering the sharpness of our vision in childhood should teach us this. What we all require is the child's sense of wonder, the simple childlikeness to worship before the magnificence of creation.

Simplicity is not necessarily easy. One of the difficulties for

1. Mat. 5:3

26

people who want to learn to meditate is just this. They ask, 'What do you have to do to meditate?' When they are told that you have to sit still and you have to learn just to say one word or one short phrase, people are often scandalized. I have had people say to me, 'Well, I've got a Ph.D. in Advanced Physics or Comparative Religion. That might be all right for the common people but for me, there must be something a little more demanding than that.' But that is the essence of meditation, to learn to be silent, to learn to be still and to learn that revelation comes in penetrating to the roots of things, to the silent roots.

Meditation is a way of breaking through from a world of illusion into the pure light of reality. The experience of meditation is that of becoming anchored in Truth, in the Way and in Life. In the Christian vision that anchor is Jesus. He reveals to us that God is the ground of our being, that none of us have any existence outside of him, that he is the Way, the Truth and Life. The great illusion that most of us are caught in is that we are the centre of the world and that everything and everyone revolves around us. Getting our Ph.D.s can serve to confirm us in that illusion. But in meditation we learn that this is not the truth. The truth is that God is the centre and everyone of us has being from his gift, from his power and from his love. Now this doesn't happen over night and, as I have suggested to you, to learn to meditate you must return to it every day, every morning and every evening, and during your meditation you must learn to recite your word from beginning to end.

The experience of meditation is that we are gradually made free. Meditation is the great way of liberation. For example, we are liberated from the past because in our meditation, we let it go when we say our word. We become open to the present through the discipline of saying the word. Thus we learn to be more and more open to our life in the present moment. The fears and regrets of the past lose their power to dominate us. We are no longer dominated by them because we are securely inserted in Being. In meditation we learn that we are because God is. We learn that simply being is our greatest gift. By being open to it, we become rooted in the ground of our being. Similarly, we are liberated from the future, from worry or from

27

fear. Indeed what we learn in meditation is that in the power of Christ we are liberated from all fear. Fear itself is the greatest obstacle between us and reality. The Christian vision has this to show each of us – that the great power that dispels all fear is love. The heart of the Christian message is that God is love and that Jesus has delivered us from the slavery of fear and has brought each of us into the light and love of God.

What each of us is invited to be open to is the capacity to enter into the very experience of Jesus himself. In the Christian revelation he has broken through the veil of fear and limitation. His risen life has opened up the way for us to enter into the pure light of reality, the pure light of love. What we learn in meditation is that this isn't just theology or theological poetry but that this is the present, living reality that is at the centre of our being. But to enter the Way as a way of Light, a way of Love, a way of limitless Life requires openness, generosity and simplicity on our part. Above all, it requires commitment. Not commitment to a cause or to an ideology but commitment in our own lives to the simplicity of the daily return to the roots of our own existence, a commitment to respond to life with attention, to create the space in our own lives to live fully. What we learn in meditation, in the silence of it and the simplicity of it, is that we have nothing to fear from the commitment to creating this space.

I think all of us fear commitment because it seems to be a reducing of our options. We say to ourselves, 'Well, if I commit myself to meditating, then I'll not be able to do other things.' But I think what all of us find is that this fear dissolves in the actual commitment to be serious, to be open, to live not out of the shallows of our being, but out of its depths. What we all find in the experience of meditation is that our horizons are expanding not contracting and we find not constraint but liberty.

How does this happen? I think it happens as a result of our commitment, not to an abstract ideal or to an ideology but to simplicity, the simplicity that is required to sit down every morning, to close our eyes and to recite the one word from beginning to end. Begin your day like this, out of the essence of your own nature. Prepare for your day by being. Then in the evening return and give meaning to everything you have done during the day by similarly being open to your own root-edness in God and open to the ground of your own being.

The mantra will lead you into a greater silence. The silence leads you to greater depth. In the depth you find not ideals or ideologies but a person who is God, who is Love. The Way is the way of simplicity. What we have to learn in meditation is to accept to be more and more simple every day of our lives. Listen to the words of Jesus again:

How blessed are those who know that they are poor; the kingdom of heaven is theirs. . . . How blessed are those whose hearts are pure; they shall see God.[2]

Meditation is the way to purity of heart, leaving behind all fear and all limitation and entering – simply – into God's presence.

2. Mat. 5:3, 8

The Way of Liberation

Some of you will have been meditating for long enough now
for me to try to say something about the way that meditation
leads us. I want to say a few words about meditation as a
commitment to reality. I am sure you know from your own
experience so far that meditation doesn't allow us to play any
games. If we are committed to saying the mantra from the
beginning to the end, and if we are committed to it absolutely
on a daily basis in our life, every morning and every evening,
then as we continue we are more and more profoundly
committed to, and open to, reality: the reality of our own
being, the reality of all creation and the reality of God. The
truly religious man or woman is the one who lives their life
responding to reality. Not to goals, not to ambitions, not to
secondary things, not to material things, not to what is trivial.
We know only too well that if we respond to what is trivial we
ourselves are trivialized.

Let me give you an example. The great illusion that we all
start with is that we are at the centre of reality. This is a very
easy illusion to fall into because in the opening consciousness
of life it seems that we are understanding the external world
from our own centre. And we seem to be monitoring the
outside world from an interior control centre. And so it seems
as though the world is revolving around us. Then logically we
begin to try to control that world, to dominate it and to put it
at our service. This is the way to alienation, to loneliness, to
anxiety because it is fundamentally unreal.

What we find in meditation, from our own experience, is
that God is the Centre. God is the Source of all reality. What
we discover, from our own experience, is that there is nothing
real outside God. Only illusion exists outside the real centre.

30

In meditation we find the courage to live in the clear light of that centre and of the reality that is God. The reality that is his creation and the reality that is my being created by God emerges from this. The result is that in meditation and through our commitment to it we become anchored in Truth. We become anchored firstly in the Way, the pilgrimage of meditation. Most importantly of all, we become anchored in Life. Our lifeline is clear. We are anchored in God. We begin to know, from our own experience that he is the ground of our being. In him we live. Through him we live. And with him we live.

What is required is commitment, perseverance. The result is that our meditation becomes the way of liberation. We are made free to *be* in the present moment, to accept fully the gift of our creation, to be fully in the eternal NOW of God. As I am sure you know from your own experience this commitment to being and to living fully in the present moment becomes a commitment to live fully every moment of your life. The reason is not hard to understand. The reason is that in meditation we are open to the Life Source within us. Once we are open to it the Life Source flows in our inmost being at every moment of our lives. In essence this is what Christianity is about. This is what Jesus came to proclaim – 'that men may have life and have it in all its fullness'.[1] In other words, we don't need to apologize for being, to make excuses for being. We don't need to spend our lives making ourselves acceptable to others. We need only to be rooted in reality and then to stand still in the ground of our own being, to live out of the power of the reality of our own being.

Meditation is a way of liberation from all fear. Fear is the greatest impediment to fullness of life. The wonder of the vision proclaimed by Jesus is that the great power of love which dispels fear is the power that we make contact with in the depths of our own being. The power of love is the energy that sweeps all before it. What we need to understand and what we need to proclaim if we are going to proclaim the Christian message to the world is that in prayer we begin to live fully

1. John 10:10

31

from the life force that is set free in our inmost being and that life force is love because it is God.

This requires commitment to life and to love. This is the commitment that Jesus proclaimed with his own life and with his own love. We must understand from our own experience that this life and love are a present reality to be found and contacted within each of us, within the heart of each one of us. This is something we must learn from our own experience. It is not enough to know from other people's experience that the Spirit of Christ dwells in our hearts and that in our hearts the living Christ summons each of us to fullness of life. That is what we must be, committed to knowing ourselves and committed to living in the power of Christ.

There are no half measures. You can't decide to do a bit of meditation. The option is to meditate and to root your life in reality. The reality is the reality of liberty – that you are freed to be, and to be fully, every moment of your life. As far as I can understand it, that is what the Gospel is about. That is what Christian prayer is about. A commitment to life, a commitment to *eternal* life. Jesus taught that the kingdom of heaven is here and now. What we have to do is to be open to it, which is to be committed to it. Listen to Jesus' words in the Gospel of Matthew:

> The kingdom of heaven is like treasure lying buried in a field. The man who found it, buried it again; and for sheer joy went and sold everything he had, and bought that field.
>
> Here is another picture of the kingdom of heaven: A merchant, looking out for fine pearls, found one of very special value, so he went and sold everything he had and bought it.[2]

This is the sort of commitment that we need – the commitment to meditate every day and in our meditation, to say the mantra from the beginning to the end.

2. Mat. 13:44–6

Beyond Illusion

To understand anything about meditation you have to find your way to a certain simplicity. In the world we live in we are so used to placing our hope and our faith in complexity. But I think all of us know, at a deeper level of our being, that real peace is to be found in a profound simplicity of spirit. These words of St Paul writing to the Ephesians need to sink into our hearts;

> Your world was a world without hope and without God. But now, in union with Christ Jesus, you who were once far off have been brought near through the shedding of Christ's blood. For he is himself our peace.[1]

One of the things that we are all invited to know from our own experience is that we *have* been brought near, through the life and death and resurrection of Jesus, to this profound peace. Aristotle defined peace as the 'tranquillity of order'. Peace and order are necessary for all growth. They are necessary for the depth of being, necessary for all of us to realize our full potential. So peace could be described as 'the harmony of directed energy'. That is what meditation is about. It isn't about passive stillness. It is about the realization of the nearness of each of us to the source of creation, the source of our own creation and of all creation. It is realizing that the power of creation, the energy of creation flows in our hearts.

The enemy of peace is distraction. We are distracted when we lose sight of the harmonizing goal of our life, the harmonizing power within which we have our being. We can lose sight

1. Eph. 2:12–14

33

of it. And we can regain it. Distraction is caused by desire, by the wish to possess. The loss of the goal leads us away from what is real into unreality.

Remember again the way of meditating. We sit down, we sit with our spine upright, we breathe calmly and regularly and we begin to say our word, *maranatha*. Four equally stressed syllables, 'Ma-ra-na-tha'. We say our mantra from the beginning to the end of our meditation. The purpose of the word is to keep us on the path, to take us away from illusion, from desire, into the reality that is God. As long as we are on the way, as long as we are saying our mantra, we are turning aside from distraction and we are on the way to make contact with the root from which we are sprung.

Once we lose sight of our goal we become confused. We become frightened. That is when we tend to seek solace in more and more distraction and illusion. What the way of meditation invites all of us to do is to confront the unreality, fear, fantasy and distraction and to pass through it. On the other side of all this illusion and fear and unreality is peace, the tranquillity of order. Energy directed to its ultimate end. What each of us is called to know in meditation is that that energy is love. What each of us is invited to discover from our own experience, is that God is love.

As I have suggested to you, meditation has nothing to do with quiet reverie. It is to do with wakefulness. We awaken to our nearness to God. All our power and all our potential is then directed towards their true end. That end is God, the end who is our beginning. In the experience of the peace of meditation it is revealed to us where we are. It is revealed to us that we are on the journey away from fear, away from unreality, away from illusion into the only reality there is. That Reality is God. That Reality is Love.

Each of us has to learn to say our word, our mantra. We have to learn to say it from the beginning of our meditation until the end, to root it in our hearts so that we can listen to it sounding there, in the depth of our being. Learning to root the mantra takes time. If you ask yourselves, 'How much time will it take?' you can answer by saying that 'it takes only that amount of time to realize that it takes no time at all'. We are already there. Listen to St Paul again: 'But now, in union with Christ Jesus, you who once were far off have been brought near through the shedding of Christ's blood, for he himself is our peace.' This is what we have to come to understand, to *know* in meditation. To know it as a personal experience. Our redemption *is* accomplished. The power of the Spirit *is* set free in our hearts. What prevents us from realizing this is that we are distracted. Our minds are cluttered and we must free them. This is what meditation is about. That is the importance of returning to it every morning and every evening.

Sit down and, in saying your mantra, loosen the chains, the bonds that bind you to unreality, to illusion and to fear. Understand that those bonds have no power over you, if only you are open to the experience of Jesus. His experience is that he is the beloved Son of God. What he has achieved for us is that we can be open to the self-same experience of knowing that we are sons and daughters of a loving, compassionate and understanding Father. In that experience we discover that our meaning is to be fully open to his love, wholly open to the nearness of his mysterious being which is wholly open to our own hearts, to our own centre. For in our centre he is to be found. Meditation, saying the mantra from beginning to end, saying the mantra every morning and every evening, is simply our pilgrimage to that centre where he is and where we are in him.

We Have Meaning for God

These are some remarkable words from the letter to the Colossians:

> Therefore, since Jesus was delivered to you as Christ and Lord, live your lives in union with him. Be rooted in him; be built in him; be consolidated in the faith you were taught; let your hearts overflow with thankfulness . . . For it is in Christ that the complete Being of the Godhead dwells embodied, and in him you have been brought to completion.[1]

These are words addressed to each one of us. 'Live your lives in union with him' is the Christian invitation. Not to admire from a distance, not even to worship from afar but to live 'in union'. That is the redemptive invitation that the Gospel addresses directly to each one of us.

We all come to know from our own experience that union requires selflessness, a real loss of self because in union we surrender ourselves into the greater reality of the union. In that reality each finds the other and, in finding the other, discovers his own essential personhood. We discover ourselves because in union we experience ourselves as known, loved, cherished, cared for. The Christian gospel reveals to each of us that this is precisely what we have been created for. We are made for union, for the perfection that comes to us from knowing ourselves known, from discovering ourselves 'in love'. 'Live your lives in union with him.' This is the invitation we respond to in our meditation. We respond to it, just as St Paul described it, by being 'rooted' in him, by being 'built' in him.

---

1. Col. 2:6–7, 9–10

What we each have to discover for ourselves is that God is the root from which we are sprung. He is the ground of our being. The most elementary sanity requires that we live out of this rootedness. Living our lives rooted in Christ, *knowing* ourselves rooted in him, as a daily experience in our daily return to our meditation means that we enter into a radical stability that is impervious to change, to passing, ephemeral contingency. In the silence of our meditation, we gain an experience of ourselves as beyond contingency. We know that we are and that we are in God and that in him we discover our own essential identity and unique meaning. The wonder of Christian prayer is that what we discover is that we have meaning for God. The astonishingly, barely believable thing about the Christian revelation is that our meaning is not less than *to bring perfection to God*. That is, to be so in harmony with him that we reflect back to him all the brilliance of his own glory, all the fullness of his own self-communication.

St Paul tells us that 'in him you have been brought to completion'. The Christian mystery summons each of us to enter into the divine milieu and to take our own appointed place within it. The fullness of the Godhead dwells in Christ and Christ dwells in us. In his indwelling we find our own completion. To be complete as human beings we must live this mystery not just intellectually, not just emotionally but with our full being. What the New Testament cries out to us is that the fullness of being we are summoned to dwells within our being as it is now and is realized when our being and the being of God come into full resonant harmony. Meditation invites us to enter the resonant harmony of God.

Beyond a certain point language always fails us. But we have to try to use language to direct our attention towards the mystery and its depths. The mantra takes up where language fails. It is like God's harmonic. By rooting it in our heart, every corner of our heart, every fibre of our being is open to him and every ounce of his power is channelled into us. That is why we must learn to say the mantra faithfully, continually and in ever-deepening poverty. Sainthood, wisdom, are simply names for reality. God is Real. We discover by that daily fidelity in our meditation that godliness is full sanity. Full sanity flowing from the full power of God's love. Each of us is summoned to discover that this godliness flows freely in the depths of our own heart.

The Reality that is Love

I have suggested to you that to meditate you have to learn to become really simple. This is quite a challenge to all of us who have been brought up with a modern consciousness in a scientific age. It may help to try and focus in on one particular aspect of this simplicity.

Let me stress for you again always to remember the importance of actually saying the mantra during the whole time of your meditation. This is what every modern person finds most difficult to understand and remember. When you start to meditate you find it difficult to believe that just in the process of taking the word *maranatha* and repeating it over and over again you can be on the way. When you begin you have to take that on faith. Nothing is more important if you want to come to a depth of perception and if you want to come to understand fully what the Christian vision of life is about. Nothing is more important for that than coming to the silence, stillness and discipline that the mantra leads you to. We have to begin by understanding that as clearly as we can. The necessity of meditating every morning and every evening and the necessity of saying your word, your mantra, from beginning to end.

Having understood that, you will come to understand from your own experience that meditation is not concerned with analysis. You are not analysing your own experience. You are not analysing your own feelings. Far from having anything to do with analysis meditation is concerned with synthesis, that is with coming to a full understanding and experience of the wholeness of creation, of your own wholeness and of your own integral part in the whole system of creation. In the Christian vision far from being concerned with analysis, which is the breaking down of reality into its component parts, the experi-

39

ence of meditation leads us to unity, to the building up into oneness of everything we are. Listen to St Paul:

> Therein lies the richness of God's free grace lavished upon us, imparting full wisdom and insight. He has made known to us his hidden purpose – such was his will and pleasure determined beforehand in Christ – to be put into effect when the time was ripe: namely, that the universe, all in heaven and all on earth, might be brought into a unity in Christ.[1]

That sounds inspiring when you listen to it but it is only words, verbal inspiration, unless you enter into the experience of it – unless you enter into a way of prayer, the meditation that can leave analysis behind and open your heart and mind to the great synthesis that happens in Christ, with Christ and through Christ.

In the monastic tradition meditation doesn't have us analyse differences in the various parts of the reality that we inhabit. Much more, we become aware of the correspondence between every part of creation as it is aligned upon Christ. So we are not analysing, we are not dividing, we are synthesising, we are unifying. It is the mantra that leads us to that by gradually calming down all our own self-important fixations, all our own self-regarding analysis. Once you begin that process, the invitation of the good news of the Gospel becomes a real possibility to live our lives out of an integral wholeness. I think you will discover, if you can persevere in saying the mantra, that your experience in meditation gradually becomes the experience throughout your life. Instead of approaching your life analysing, noticing the differences, you approach your life wholeheartedly, responding to the correspondences.

The way the early Christians described this was that you come to approach your life with love because what you encounter in your heart is the living principle of love. St Paul here is suggesting how we should be aligned on this principle in our relationships with one another:

> Be forbearing with one another, and forgiving, where any of

1. Eph. 1:7–10

40

you has cause for complaint: you must forgive as the Lord forgave you. To crown all, there must be love to bind all together and complete the whole.[2]

That is the new vision of life that we enter into through our meditation – completion, wholeness, unity, 'in love'. We come to know then that the greatest theological statement was made by St John when he said, 'God is love'. The great mystery of the Christian faith is that this love is to be found in your own heart if only you can be silent and still and if only you can make this love the supreme centre of all your being and action. That means turning to it wholeheartedly, paying full attention to it. It means going beyond yourself into the reality that is infinitely greater than you are and yet which contains you. And in which each of us has an essential and unique place.

In the Christian tradition the experience of prayer, the experience of meditation, is of unity, of oneness. It is an experience that changes the whole of our perception of reality. We see reality as a whole unified by the basic energy of the cosmos which is the energy of love. This is the message of the truth that sets us free.

And you too, when you had heard the message of the truth, the good news of your salvation, and had believed it, became incorporate in Christ and received the seal of the promised Holy Spirit; and that Spirit is the pledge that we shall enter upon our heritage, when God has redeemed what is his own, to his praise and glory.[3]

The most important thing that Christians have to proclaim to the world, to whoever has ears to hear, is that this Spirit does indeed dwell in our hearts and that, by turning to it with full attention, we too can live out of the fullness of love. We too can live out of this power that is the kingdom of God.

We can only proclaim what we know. The daily return to meditation is essential to knowing; this and the discipline of the mantra from beginning to end is essential. But never become

2. Col. 3:13–15   3. Eph. 1:13–14

41

discouraged or down-hearted. If unity is our goal, we all have to begin from a fairly fractured beginning. Learning to say the mantra requires great patience and demands great perseverance. Don't give up too easily. When you find that you have strayed from it, return to it immediately. Stillness of body and stillness of Spirit, this is the aim. To be totally open to the only reality that is ultimately real, the reality that is love.

The Temple of Your Heart

It is important to be aware of the danger of using the imagination when you come to think about prayer or meditation. I don't think it is any exaggeration to say that the imagination is the great enemy of prayer. This idea has been impressed on me by people I have met recently who seem to me to miss the whole point of prayer and the richness of the Christian understanding of prayer by an over-active imagination. The imaginative stories I have heard people tell of praying in a church at night, when suddenly Christ walks down the aisle to speak to them. When I ask them, 'What did he look like?' they say, 'Tall, Jewish, with flowing hair, piercing eyes . . .' and so forth . . . Now I don't question for a moment the sincerity of people who see visions of this kind, even though these visions are often caused by badly digested meals. What I want to suggest is the more important conviction of the early Church concerning the reality of the presence of Jesus within us. This is the reality of the presence of his indwelling Spirit. The real wonder of the Christian life is that each one of us is called to live out of this reality, to live out of the eternal part of our own being. The two great Christian words that refer to this living out of the eternal are meditation and contemplation.

Meditation means remaining in the centre, being rooted in the centre of your own being, and *contemplation* is being in the temple with him. The temple is your own heart, your own centre. The essence of being with him in the vision of the early Church is an absolute oneness, a oneness with the Absolute. We have to try to proclaim to the world that it is our destiny to be thus divinized by becoming one with the Spirit of God. Divinization is something utterly beyond our imagination and beyond our own powers of understanding to comprehend. But, and here is the mystery that the New Testament speaks of, it is not beyond our capacity to experience it in love. It is our capacity to love and to be rooted in love that is the essence of our divinization.

When St Paul speaks about the reality of this, he emphasizes the presentness of it. For him it was Jesus who has already brought us salvation. 'Salvation' is deliverance from all our own limitations. It is the Hebrew word for deliverance from bondage and slavery into the 'glorious liberty and splendour of the children of God'.[1]

> It is he who brought us salvation and called us to a dedicated life, not for any merit of ours but of his own purpose and of his own grace, which was granted to us in Christ Jesus from all eternity, but has now, at length, been brought fully into view by the appearance on earth of our Saviour Jesus Christ. For he has broken the power of death and brought life and immortality to light through the Gospel.[2]

The Gospel is just that 'good news' of our deliverance from slavery. If we wanted to put that into language for our own time, it is a deliverance from our own egoism, from everything in us that isolates us, limits us; all these limitations are exchanged for the limitless love of God. It is the reality of this that we must be open to in our prayer – the presentness of it. This Spirit of Christ which is pure gift, the gift of his Spirit, is the very basis of all reality. And the art of living, of all fully human living, is not to live at the surface or at the level of trivia but to live out of what Jesus called that 'inner spring' of eternal life always welling up within us.

This is the message of St Paul:

> I want them to continue in good heart and in the unity of love, and to come to the full wealth of conviction which understanding brings, and grasp God's secret. That secret is Christ himself; in him lie hidden all God's treasures of wisdom and knowledge.[3]

1. Rom. 8:21   2. 2 Tim. 1:9–10   3. Col. 2:2–3

This is possible for us because 'it is in Christ that the complete Being of the Godhead dwells embodied, and in him you have been brought to completion'.[4] That is why in our prayer, as we meditate as faithfully as we can each morning and evening, we must go beyond all imagination, beyond all thought, even holy thought and holy imagination. It is why we must be utterly still and reverent in the presence of the mystery of God, this 'inner spring', because it is out of that mystery that we are invited to live. 'Be rooted in him; be built in him; be consolidated in the faith you were taught; let your hearts overflow with thankfulness'.[5]

Let us see this clearly. Wonderful as this message is, intoxicating though it is, we must approach it with simplicity and humility. That is why we must learn to say our word and to say it with a deepening faithfulness morning and evening. We must say it without expectation, without thinking that we are going to put pressure on God or that we are going to twist his arm and make him reveal himself to us in some way. We are simply doing the most direct thing we can do if we genuinely want to live our lives to the full and to live them out of the infinite depth they possess, their infinite potentiality.

We live them in union with Christ. That is the real wonder of meditation, that we do lose ourselves because we are in the temple with him. It is in that loss of self that we find ourselves in Christ. And in him we are infinitely expanded in heart by love. We are each called to the experience that inspired St Paul to write these words to the Colossians,

> Therefore, since Jesus was delivered to you as Christ and Lord, live your lives in union with him. Be rooted in him; be built in him; be consolidated in the faith you were taught; let your hearts overflow with thankfulness . . . For it is in Christ that the complete being of the Godhead dwells embodied, and in him you have been brought to completion.[6]

4. Col. 2:9–10   5. Col. 2:7   6. Col. 2:6–7, 9

45

Rooted in the Centre

The other day I was reading of a Buddhist monk from Vietnam who was giving a talk in an American university and at the end of his talk, one of the students asked, 'Would you tell us what method of meditation you teach to the novices who come to your monastery?' His reply was, 'For the first three years the novices make the tea for the senior monks.' You can understand the wisdom of that, particularly in a society that is not dominated by time and by speed. But in our own society I think all of us have a more acute sense of urgency, that we have to do something *now* to understand the mystery of our own existence. Whereas it might well be wiser to spend three years just making tea, most of us feel that we haven't the time and we have to begin right away. That sense of urgency we have in the West can be a very great strength to us; if we act on it. In this talk I want to try to put before you something of the wisdom that is involved in coming to terms with that fundamental question of the purpose of our own existence.

A point in mathematics has position but no magnitude; it has no size. It has its place and that is all it has. What *we* have to do is to arrive at the central point of our own being. This is the purpose of meditation. The mathematical idea of the point having position but no magnitude is very descriptive of our meditation. In meditation we find our point, our position in the cosmos. And in the Christian tradition and vision of meditation each of us has our own unique place. We can describe that place in various ways. Now, I just want to suggest that that place is found when each of us is rooted in God, rooted in the centre of all creation, of all energy and of all power.

Meditation makes demands on us. It is a discipline. It isn't good enough just to read books about it or follow courses on it. You have to practise it. In the practice, you find your place. But to find your place you have to reduce yourself constantly until you become just a point. We all know that there is nothing worse than self-importance. There is nothing worse than selfishness. The purpose of meditation is to enter into our central point which is the experience of self-transcendence, a going forward. We leave self utterly behind and our ego is reduced and reduced and reduced until we have our place but no magnitude.

Coming to that point at the centre of our own being is like adjusting the aperture of a camera. When we have reduced ourself to that one-pointedness and when we are still, the light shines into us, into our hearts. That is the light of God, the light that enlightens and illuminates our entire being. Once we have achieved that pointedness and stillness the light shines in our heart for all eternity. Don't misunderstand me. To tread this path you do not require any special characteristics or special talents except the ordinary talent of knowing that we must go beyond self-importance and self-centredness. And it does not take much ingenuity to realize that. We must root ourselves not in self-love but in universal love. We become persons, not for ourselves, but for others, for all, for *the* all.

The light coming in that aperture is like a long exposure, the camera must be completely still and we must learn to be still. Before you meditate it is sometimes good to listen to a little music. The music helps you to forget the words, ideas and images that we have just been using. When the music is finished try to be as still as possible. Sit as upright as possible, close your eyes gently, and then begin to say your word, your mantra, 'Maranatha', four equally-stressed syllables. That is all we have to do for the twenty-five to thirty minutes of our meditation. Don't think about God, don't try to imagine God but simply be, be in his presence. We can be inspired to do this by what the prophet Isaiah says, 'I was there to be sought by a people who did not ask, to be found by men who did not seek me.'[1] That is the way of meditation – to be still, to be one-pointed, to be rooted in God. As St Paul, writing to the Romans, put

1. Isa. 65:1

47

it, 'Remember that it is not you who sustain the root: the root sustains you.'[2] That too is the way of meditation – to be utterly still, humble and reverent in the presence of God.

Don't worry about how the time is passing. Do not be disappointed if you find that you follow your thoughts instead of saying your mantra. Return to it, return to it gently, return to it constantly. If you want to learn to meditate, if you want to set out on this road of transcendence and one-pointedness, it is essential that you learn the practice of meditating every day of your life, every morning and every evening. The optimum time is half an hour, the minimum time is about twenty minutes. You will find that in the time of your meditation nothing happens. Say your word and be content to say your word. But in the perseverance along the way of meditation you will begin to understand the truth about one-pointedness, about centredness and from your own experience you will begin to understand what St Paul meant when he said, 'Remember that it is not you who sustain the root: the root sustains you.'

2. Rom. 11:18

Smashing the Mirror

These are some words of St Paul from the Letter to the Colossians:

> May he strengthen you, in his glorious might, with ample power to meet whatever comes with fortitude, patience and joy; and to give thanks to the Father who has made you fit to share the heritage of God's people in the realm of light.[1]

We should notice the extraordinarily positive and confident quality of those words, 'ample power'. This is exactly what Christianity is about. It is living our lives to the full out of that ample power of God and living them, as St Paul put it, with fortitude. That means living with courage, not afraid of difficulties or of ourselves or of others. Above all, not afraid of God because we are united to him as our supreme power source.

One of the misunderstandings people have about meditation arises from seeing it as something passive. They see it often in terms of surrender. This is because the words of the traditional religious vocabulary have been words like surrender, abandonment and self-forgetfulness. They have real meaning but we have to understand them in the light of the experience of the power and the joy that St Paul speaks of. I would like to suggest to you that a way for us to understand what this Christian experience is about and the way to enter it in meditation is not so much surrender or abandonment but *empathy* with God. To use a contemporary analogy, it is like getting on to the same wavelength. All the essential ideas of St Paul have this sense of resonating on the same frequency with Christ. He calls it

1. Col. 1:11–12

union with the power source. What prevents that union, that co-resonance?

The only thing that can prevent it is what we might describe as self-consciousness, the hyper-self-consciousness of egoism. I do not think it is any exaggeration to say that original sin is self-consciousness, because self-consciousness gives rise to the divided consciousness. This is like having a mirror between God and ourselves. Every time we look into the mirror we see ourselves. The purpose of meditation is to smash that mirror so that we no longer look at reflections of things and consequently see everything backwards, including yourself. The essence of meditation is taking the kingdom of heaven by storm. The mirror must be smashed. And Jesus is talking about overcoming self-consciousness, the mirroring self, when he says no one can be a follower of his unless he leaves self behind.

Now it does not take very much knowledge of life to perceive that this self-consciousness deludes us into seeing the whole universe revolve around us; or to conclude that this self-consciousness is an appalling state to be in. Perhaps that is what brings most of us to meditation. We don't want to look into that mirror and see everything backwards for the rest of our lives. We want to look through it, beyond it, and beyond ourselves. We want to look with courage into the infinite mystery of God. But when we begin to feel that first loss of self-consciousness and when we begin to enter into the deep silence of meditation we can become disturbed and take fright. This is where we need the support of brethren. That is why our regular meetings are so important. We need to realize that faith is a gift – given to us, as St Paul tells us, in abundance if only we will be open to it and continue hammering at that mirror until it shatters utterly. We hammer at it with our mantra.

There is nothing passive whatsoever about meditation. It is a state of growing and deepening openness with the power source of all reality which we can only adequately describe in words as God-who-is-love. The aim of our life and the invitation of our life is nothing less than complete union, full resonance with that power source. What are the fruits of un-self-consciousness? Joy, love, peace, self-control, patience, fidelity

– all the things that St Paul speaks about as the fruits of the spirit. This is the state of being where we are free to be ourselves, free to receive the gift of our life without fear, in the state of grace, of love.

St Paul mentions patience in that list of spiritual gifts. Each one of us must learn patience and there is no greater school of patience than the willingness faithfully to recite your mantra day after day, unconcerned with progress, unconcerned with results, aware that there is only the pilgrimage. If we are not on the pilgrimage, we are nowhere. Our call and our destiny is to be in Christ.

Meditation is about openness to that 'ample power' of God. It brings us to the confidence of knowing that we can meet whatever comes, not out of our own resources or our own self-consciousness but out of *the* consciousness of Christ, his consciousness of his Father and our Father. That consciousness is to be found in our hearts beyond all mirrors, beyond all images. That consciousness is not threatening. That consciousness is the gentle power of Jesus Christ.

The Way to the Eternal

One of the questions all meditators have to face is, 'Why do we meditate?' I suppose none of us would meditate unless it had occurred to us that there was more to life than just being producers or consumers. All of us know that we can't find any enduring or ultimate meaning in just producing and consuming. So we seek that ultimate meaning. We come to meditation because an unerring instinct tells us that if we can't find any ultimate satisfaction in consuming or producing nor can we find ultimate meaning outside of ourselves. We have to *begin with* ourselves.

In our society a lot of people, faced with the problem of being, living and meaning, seek refuge in oblivion. It is summed up in the expression, 'being stoned out of your mind'. And Marx, one of the most formative influences on the society in which we live, saw religion as the opium of the people. There is a real sense in which we can turn to religion as an anaesthetic, to be comforted or to be put into a state of unconsciousness. But Christian meditation has nothing to do with anaesthesia. Meditation is the way to illumination, to light and to life. Christ's message is one of vitalization and illumination, complete enlightenment. The way to this is the way of single-mindedness, not being distracted by things that are passing away but ever more deeply committed to what is enduring, to what is eternal.

Our own spirit is enduring. Our own spirit is eternal in God.

That is all right as an intellectual insight, as a religious insight or even a religious conviction. But the call of Christianity is the authenticating call of every truly spiritual doctrine – to be open yourself to your own eternal spirit, open to your own rootedness in the Eternal. Start to tread the way, the pilgrimage to fullness of light and fullness of meaning. Now what is the way?

It is the way of poverty and simplicity, because the way to fullness of knowledge is the way of unlearning. Let me remind you again of the way of meditation. Sit down and sit still, close your eyes and begin to say your word, 'Maranatha'. Say the word deliberately yet relaxedly, say it faithfully and yet serenely – four syllables all equally stressed, 'Ma-ra-na-tha'.

We say the word because the pilgrimage is a pilgrimage beyond ourselves, beyond our own limitations. To go beyond ourselves we must transcend thought and imagination, and the word is the way, the vehicle that carries us forward. The challenge of meditation is to undertake the discipline of saying the word and continuing to say it while learning to be patient, learning how to wait and learning that the way forward is the way to our own centre. The way to enduring riches is the way of poverty. The way to enlightenment is the way of darkness. We have to go through with ever greater discipline, with ever greater faithfulness.

But we must understand this – the way is simple. It is wholly uncomplicated. The way is sure. All that is required is the daily return to it – not with demands or any materialistic measuring of success. Just simple faithfulness, simple poverty of spirit. Every morning and every evening devoting your time not to what is passing but to what is enduring: your own spirit alive and full of light in God. We have an amazing call. Listen to it described in the second letter to the Thessalonians:

We are bound to thank God for you, brothers [and sisters] beloved by the Lord, because from the beginning of time God chose you to find salvation in the Spirit that consecrates you, and in the truth that you believe. It was for this that he called you through the gospel we brought, so that you might possess for your own the splendour of our Lord Jesus Christ.[1]

1. 2 Thess. 2:13–14

Original Innocence

When we have just celebrated one of the great feasts of the Church I think we have a good opportunity to reassess our own commitment. None of us can be unmoved when, for example, we enter into the liturgy of Good Friday and are confronted with the faithfulness and dedication of Christ. None of us can experience the joy of Easter morning, the universal promise of the new life of the Resurrection without again understanding in the centre of our being that there *is* new life, a re-creation around us at all times. This is a good moment for us to understand our own commitment to meditation, our own commitment to prayer as giving quality to our whole life by finding meaning and purpose in living in our prayer, by discovering Christ in our own heart.

I would like to try to redefine for you or to reclarify what meditation is about. When we sit down to meditate and turn our minds away from thinking and imagining, away from thinking about ourselves or about God, what we are doing is entering into the centre of our own being. The purpose of saying the one word during meditation, the one phrase, the mantra, is that each of us can become wholly still at the centre of our being.

The call of Jesus is to maturity. The whole thrust of St Paul is that we become mature in Christ. In all nature, growth is from the centre outwards. The centre is where we begin. This is the experience of meditation as we return to it day after day. There is no short-cut, we must meditate every morning and every evening of our lives precisely because this is the most central of all activities in our life. The experience of growth is of returning to our origin, to our centre, to God. St John of the Cross described it most beautifully when he said, 'God is the centre of my soul'.

As modern men and women we are much influenced by the concept of progress. But I think we must understand that progress does not consist so much in leaving our origin but much more in realizing all the potential in our origin, which we do by returning to our origin. All growth that endures in nature must be thoroughly rooted, and it is the summons of each one of us to be thoroughly rooted in Christ. I think there is a real sense in which meditation is a return to our original innocence. The Fathers describe this way as 'purity of heart'. The call of each one of us from Jesus is to find our own heart and to find it unclouded by egoism, unclouded by images, unclouded by desire. Meditation leads us to the clarity that comes from original and eternal simplicity. So we are content simply to be with him, content simply and in a childlike way to say our word, our one word, from the beginning to the end of our meditation.

To begin to meditate requires nothing more than the determination to begin. To begin to discover our roots, to begin to discover our potential, to begin to return to our source. And God is our source. In the simplicity of meditation beyond all thought and imagination we begin to discover in utter simplicity that we are in God; we begin to understand that we are in God in whom we live and move and have our being. We try to describe this growing awareness that we discover in the silence and daily commitment as 'undivided consciousness'. Meditation is just this state of simplicity that is the fully mature development of our original innocence. As St Catherine of Genoa expressed it, 'My me is God. Nor do I know myself save in him.' The wonder of the proclamation of Christianity is that everyone of us is invited into this same state of simple, loving union with God. This is what Jesus came both to proclaim and to achieve. This is what each of us is invited to be open to. 'My me is God. Nor do I know myself save in him.'

And how do we know this? We know it because, as St Paul expresses it, 'We possess the mind of Christ'.[1] This sentence of

1. 1 Cor. 2:16

St Paul is one of the most extraordinary sentences in Christian revelation. As I have said before, if we Christians have a fault, it is that we are so blind to the extraordinary riches that are already ours, achieved for us, given to us by Jesus. We possess the mind of Christ – Christ who knows the Father and who knows us. This is what each of us is invited to discover from our own experience – that we know because we are known and that we love because we are loved. St John writes, 'The love I speak of is not our love for God, but the love he showed to us in sending his Son'.[2] All great truths are simplicity itself. We can only know them when we become simple. When we sit down to meditate and begin to say our word, our mantra, we are on our way to that simplicity. We are on our way to the foundation on which our whole being rests. We are on our way to union, union with Jesus. We are on our way with him to the Father.

This was and is the inspiration of the words of St Paul:

Among men, who knows what a man is but that man's own spirit within him? In the same way, only the Spirit of God knows what God is. This is the Spirit that we have received from God, and not the spirit of the world, so that we may know all that God of his own grace has given us.[3]

That is the invitation given to every one of us so that we may know personally from our own experience all that God of his own grace gives us. The way to that knowledge is the way of faithfulness, a daily faithfulness to our meditation. Faithfully every morning and every evening of our lives to turn aside from everything that is passing away and to be open to the eternal Spirit of God. It is also the way of faithfulness during our meditation, faithfully to say our word, our mantra, from beginning to end, no following of thoughts, no spinning of phrases or words; in growing simplicity. The power by which we do all this is given to us. It is the power of the love of Jesus. As St Paul calls each of us to know: 'Surely you know that you are God's temple, where the Spirit of God dwells.'[4] In our

2. 1 John 4:10   3. 1 Cor. 2:11–12   4. 1 Cor. 3:16

meditation we seek to be as fully open as we can be in this life to the Spirit of God dwelling within us.

Simplicity is Oneness

We can always find new ways to describe what meditation is really about. But remember always to keep clear in your minds how you meditate. That is, you take your word, your mantra, and you begin to recite it at the beginning of your meditation and you keep it going through the meditation. You must never lose contact with the fundamental simplicity of that. There is always a danger that in thinking or talking about meditation we can use so many superlatives that we lose contact with its essential simplicity which is, of course, the essential simplicity of simply saying the mantra. In that is the purification of our whole being.

I want to try to describe to you what this purification is that we are undertaking when we meditate. I want to suggest that meditation is simply a way of coming to your own centre and remaining in your centre awake, alive and still. The great problem with the lives of so many of us is that we live at an incredibly shallow level. By meditating we seek to find our way to the depths of our own being. The word 'meditation' comes from the Latin *meditare* which breaks down into the roots *stare in medio* – to remain in the centre. The word 'contemplation' suggests the same. The word contemplation does not mean looking at anything – God or anyone else. Contemplation is 'being in the temple' with God. The temple is your own heart, the depths of your own being.

By meditating we leave the shallow levels of our life behind and enter into something that is profound. By meditating we leave behind the passing, ephemeral things of life and enter into what is eternal.The ultimate goal of all religion is a *re-linking* and it is essentially the re-linking with our own deep centre. To be re-linked to our own centre is the purpose of all religion. We know from the Christian revelation that the Spirit of God dwells in our own centre, in the depths of our own spirit. The truth we discover from our own experience, if only we will tread the pilgrimage to that place of holiness, is that there is only one centre and that that centre is everywhere.

What I think each one of us has to discover from our own experience in order to come alive is that this pilgrimage is the first responsibility of our lives. It is the first responsibility of every life that would be fully human – to return to our own centre and to live out of the depths of our own profound capacity for life. We then discover that being reconnected with our own centre reconnects us with every centre. The truly spiritual man or woman learns first of all to live in harmony with themselves and then to live in harmony with the whole of creation. What we can say is, 'To be in one's own centre is to be in God.' Or in the words of Jesus, 'The kingdom of heaven is within you.'[1] We must remember that this kingdom is not a place but an experience. It is the wholly integrated and integrating experience of the reality of the power of God. And in the Christian vision it is knowing that that power is the power of love.

When St John of the Cross said, 'God is the centre of my soul,' it was because at the centre we experience silence, utter stillness and the peace that is beyond all understanding. The way to this is the way of the mantra. We should be very practical. In meditating we seek to enter into an ever more profound simplicity. As I said in the first of these talks, the way is the way of unlearning. The way is the way of dispossession. The way is the way of simplicity. We unlearn and we dispossess ourselves by turning aside from all our own words and thoughts and staying solely with the mantra. That is what takes us to the depths. What all of us must understand is that you can't just do a bit of meditation. If you want to meditate then you have to place it in a central position in your life and you have to make sure that everything in your life is in harmony with the harmony you come to find in your own spirit. You cannot live, as it were, a double life and only in one half be

1. Luke 17:21

59

a harmonious, integrated person, on your way to depth, to enlightenment and to profound vitalization. You have to be a simple person. You have to be a person who is living the oneness in your own life. Simplicity is oneness.

These words of St Peter say something that all of us have to listen to carefully, because the problem for people in our own time in learning to meditate is to have a sufficient grasp of their own potentiality as well as a firm enough belief that they really can live out of depths profounder than the shallowness of every day. These words of St Peter are a call to us to recognize who we are, to recognize our own dignity, to recognize the wonder of our own being and to recognize above all our own lovableness.

So come to him, our living Stone – the stone rejected by men but choice and precious in the sight of God. Come, and let yourselves be built, as living stones, into a spiritual temple; become a holy priesthood, to offer spiritual sacrifices acceptable to God through Jesus Christ . . . you are a chosen race, a royal priesthood, a dedicated nation, and a people claimed by God for his own, to proclaim the triumphs of him who has called you out of darkness into his marvellous light.[2]

2. 1 Pet. 2:4–5, 9

Beyond Technique

One of the great problems about learning to meditate is that it is so simple. In the sort of society that we live in we are not used to putting our total trust and faith in something that is very, very simple. We have all been brought up to trust only complex things. So when we approach something like meditation, we tend to get interested in the techniques that are involved. The techniques have their place. But they are not the first thing to turn your mind to when you are learning to meditate. The most important thing when you are beginning is to understand the absolute simplicity of it. Then, remain faithful to the simplicity of the practice.

When we begin to meditate we take our place in a great tradition. We are not just starting on something new to which we are bringing all the elements of new-found knowledge. We are entering a tradition of hundreds, indeed of thousands of years. When we begin we have to be humble enough to accept the tradition. We have to accept it on faith. This is our tradition as Benedictine monks – to meditate you must learn to *be* still. You must learn to sit absolutely still in your bodily presence and you must move towards an interior stillness in your spirit. The way into this that we have from the tradition passed on from our great monastic teacher, John Cassian, is to take a very simple word or phrase and just repeat it over and over again. The word I suggest that you take is the word *maranatha*. Say the mantra as gently as you can. Use no force but move towards absolute fidelity. To learn to meditate it is necessary to meditate every morning and every evening every day of your life; and it is necessary to repeat the mantra from the beginning to the end.

Meditation is the way of becoming wholly present to God by

coming to understand the fullness of the mystery of life. Most of us in our sort of society think of God, indeed think of ourselves as a sort of problem. God is a problem that we have to solve. Our life is a problem we have to solve. And to solve the problem you need an adequate technique. But what the tradition of meditation has to tell us is that God is not a problem, nor is our life a problem. God is a mystery and our own life is a mystery. In the presence of mystery what we must do is let the mystery be. Allow the mystery the fullness of its own being. Allow it to reveal itself. When we meditate that is exactly what we do. We allow God to be God. We allow ourselves to *be* in his presence. That is the extraordinary power of it.

Chronologically, the first thing we have to do is to become fully present to ourselves. That is why absolute stillness of mind and spirit is necessary. For many of us, it will be the first experience we have had of the totality of our being. What we do when we meditate is enter fully into the present moment and each time you recite your mantra, you are wholly present to that moment. You are not thinking of the past, you are not planning for the future. You are there, totally in that moment. Jesus is always calling on us to wake up. 'Can't you wake up? Be awake.' In meditation we learn to wake up to the reality of our existence and the reality of God.

There is nothing more maddening than talking to a person who is only half listening to you. Someone was telling me the other day that they were talking to someone about the terrible problem of starvation in part of East Africa. The conversation took place over some coffee and when the first person who was talking about the starvation was half way through and paused the person she was talking to said, 'How many eggs have you put into this cake? It's delicious.' That is an example of the maddening frustration of being with someone who is only half present to you. The gospels show how exasperated Jesus became with such people.

What Jesus tells us is that there is nothing worse than being half awake (or half asleep). When you sleep, sleep fully and when you are awake, come to full wakefulness. And that is what our meditation leads us to. By becoming wholly present in *this* moment, in the moment when we say our mantra, we enter into the Eternal Now of God. The principal criticism one might have of contemporary Christians is that we are and have been so slow to understand the full, present magnificence of the invitation that we have to be wholly open to Christ. St Paul writing to the Corinthians of this invitation to life says, 'It is God himself who has called you to share in the life of his Son Jesus Christ Our Lord; and God keeps faith.'[1] The tradition tells us that the life, the power of God, the power of his love is to be found in our own hearts. Finding that power requires that we be totally present to it. The tradition also tells us that our call is to become wholly awake to this mystery and to awaken to it as a mystery of wholeness. We discover ourselves by losing ourselves in the Other, and only then can we discover our essential place in the total mystery of Reality.

Most modern people, as a result of the philosophies of the last two or three hundred years, have thought of this as an invitation to come merely to the knowledge of their own limited or individual being. But what the Christian tradition reminds us is that our invitation is something much greater than that. It is to find our place, our insertion point in a Reality that is infinitely greater not only than each of us but of the sum total of all of us. The invitation is to find ourselves wholly alive within the mystery of God. The task we face is to become simple enough, humble enough simply to say our word, simply to return to saying our word and leaving behind all thought and imagination at the time of meditation. Remember, of course, that there are other times for reflection, for analysis, but those times are not the times of meditation. During the time of meditation we must learn to be like little children, to be spiritually childlike, which is to be content with saying our word and letting go of all thought, imagination and analysis.

When we meditate we are like the eye that looks forward into the mystery of Being and, like the eye, we cannot see ourselves. But we can *see* and our invitation *is* to see. The way is the way of meditation as a way of silence, a way of simplicity, of humility and above all, the way of the mantra. Learning to

1. 1 Cor. 1:9

say the mantra to the exclusion of everything else. Say it, recite it, listen to it. This is how we respond to the call addressed to each of us by 'God himself': thank God for all the enrichment that has come to you in Christ. In him you possess full knowledge and you can give full expression to it. There is no single gift you lack. 'It is God himself who called you to share in the life of his Son Jesus Christ Our Lord; and God keeps faith.'

Death

A question that all societies in every time and place have exercised their minds about is the question of death. All people who have a serious approach to life see death as a moment of supreme importance for all of us. Yet, in the Christian vision, death is not the all-important moment in our life. That is, not if we have listened to what Jesus has to say to us or if we have listened to what the revelations of the early Christians have to say to us – and if we have acted upon these. This is what I want to reflect on now.

For St Paul, the supreme all-important moment in any life is the moment of full openness to Jesus. Openness to his power, openness to his glory. That moment is an eternal moment. Nothing subsequent to it can fundamentally shake us from what he describes as the rootedness in Christ which grows out of this moment. For Paul, Jesus is the revelation of God and he is the revelation of his glory in our own heart. The call of the Christian life is simply to be open to that glory. The whole purpose of our life is a pilgrimage to that moment. As I have often said to you, the only ultimate thing of significance for each of us is that we *are* on the pilgrimage. The moment of revelation is given in God's time. What we have to do is to tread the way of poverty, of obedience and of simplicity. To be ready. The danger of Christian life is that we can become so easily intoxicated by the sheer wonder of the proclamation that we don't take the practical steps necessary to put ourselves into readiness.

All my life I have met with people who are intoxicated by the sheer beauty of the Christian vision but who undergo that intoxication from a distance. Entering into the eternal life of that moment seems to them impossible. Yet, the whole proclamation of the early Church is that everyone of us is invited to this. We are invited to it as the supreme opportunity of our life. We needn't think about our 'obligation' to worship God if we can understand something of the pure gift of his communication of this life to us. Even if we can understand in only the most elementary way that Jesus is this vital principle within each of us, then we are already opening our minds to the wonder of what St Paul calls the 'glory', the 'splendour' of God.

What is equally clear from the New Testament is that Jesus achieved his mission by total abandonment of self, by handing over his life to the Father: 'Not my will but thy will be done.' That is exactly the way for all of us. And it is the precise purpose of all meditation. To lose our lives, to lose ourselves and to become totally absorbed in God through the human consciousness of Jesus is what gives meaning to death, because it gives ultimate meaning to life. Meditation is a powerful way if you can learn to say the mantra continually, ceaselessly, because that is the way in prayer to leave self behind, to lay down our life so as to be absorbed in the infinite mystery of God. People ask, 'What is the experience of prayer?' The experience of prayer is of going utterly beyond ourselves, going beyond any words that we could possibly use to describe the experience. St Paul describes it as the entry into the glory of God. But in saying our mantra we leave behind all the words, because they limit the experience. They make the experience self-reflective. The experience is one of infinity, and no finite word can possibly encompass the experience. But again let me stress for you the way is the way of simplicity and childlikeness. 'Unless you become like children . . .' means unless you find again in your own heart the capacity for wonder, for innocent wonder, an innocence we all lose so easily and so carelessly. But we must find it again. The way we find it is to enter into silence, to be, to be open to God's glory, to the wonder of his being. That is why our mantra is of such supreme importance. That is why day-dreaming is such a dreadful loss of opportunity, such a dreadful encapsulation in time. Whereas all of us are called into that eternal moment when we lose ourselves in God.

Listen to St Paul again,

We are bound to thank God always for you, brothers beloved by the Lord, because from the beginning of time God chose you to find salvation in the Spirit that consecrates you, and in the truth that you believe. It was for this that he called you through the gospel which we brought, so that you might possess for your own the splendour of our Lord Jesus Christ.[1]

Those words give us some idea of what the invitation is – salvation in the Spirit. Salvation in the Spirit means being taken utterly beyond ourselves into supreme liberty of being in the Spirit of God. We are called to that now. 'The kingdom of heaven is among you.' We are called to it in the most practical way – to take our day and to put eternal life in the first place of our day. It is in eternal life that we turn definitively from death and dying. The only ultimate tragedy is a life that has not opened to eternal life. The only ultimate tragedy is a life that is dying.

1. 2 Thess. 2:13–14

Death and Resurrection

St Benedict told his monks, 'Always keep death before your eyes.'[1] We don't talk much about death in the modern world. But what the whole Christian tradition tells us is that if we would become wise we must learn the lesson that we have here 'no abiding city'. Our life begins, develops, matures and then we must prepare for the end of this mortal life. What the wise men of ages past and present say to us is that to have life in focus we must have death in our field of vision. Death is important because it reminds us of the fragility of the human condition. Our awareness of it is the constant reminder of the mortality of life. This knowledge of death is the source of compassion, of forgiveness, of gentleness, because death makes each one of us aware of our own weakness and mortality. We can be noble in the face of death but it is hard to be proud. So death is important because it teaches us compassion and humility. It is in the compassionate and humble heart that the power of God reaches us. 'When I am weak, then I am strong.'[2]

Talking about death is hard for the worldly to understand. Indeed the principal fantasy of much worldliness operates out of completely the opposite point of view: not the wisdom of our own mortality but the pure fantasy that we are immortal, beyond physical weakness. But the wisdom of the tradition of which St Benedict is the spokesman, is that awareness of our physical weakness enables us to see our own spiritual fragility too. There is a profound awareness in all of us, so profound indeed that it is often buried for much of the time, that we must make contact with the fullness of life and the source of life. We must make contact with the power of God and

1. Rule of St Benedict, ch. 4   2. 2 Cor. 12:10

somehow, open our own fragile 'earthen vessels' to the eternal love of God, the love that cannot be quenched. All of us know, if only dimly at this deep level, that our mortal bodies do need this new life of love. Indeed, we know that this is what we were created for. Meditation is our way to full awakening on this level of profoundity when we meet the basic truth about the human condition, that each of us was created for infinite expansion of mind and heart.

Meditation is a way of power because it is the way to understand our own mortality. It is the way to get our own death into focus. It can do so because it is the way beyond our own mortality. It is the way beyond our own death to the resurrection, to a new and eternal life, the life that arises from our union with God. The essence of the Christian gospel is that we are invited to this experience now, today. All of us are invited to death, to die to our own self-importance, our own selfishness, our own limitations. We are invited to die to our own exclusiveness. We are invited to all this because Jesus has died before us and has risen from the dead. Our invitation to die is also one to rise to new life, to community, to communion, to a full life without fear. I suppose it would be difficult to estimate what it is people fear most – death or resurrection. But in meditation we lose all our fear because we realize that death is death to fear and resurrection is rising to new life.

Every time we sit down to meditate we enter this axis of death and resurrection. We do so because in our meditation we go beyond our own life and all the limitations of our own life into the mystery of God. We discover, each of us from our own experience, that the mystery of God is the mystery of love, infinite love – love that casts out all fear. This is our resurrection, our rising to the full liberty that dawns on us once our own life and death and resurrection are in focus. Meditation is the great way of focusing our life on the eternal reality that is God, the eternal reality that is to be found in our own hearts. The discipline of saying the mantra, the discipline of the daily return morning and evening to meditation has this one supreme aim – to focus us totally on Christ with an acuity of vision that sees ourselves, all reality as it is.

Listen to St Paul writing to the Romans:

No one of us lives, and equally no one of us dies, for himself alone. If we live we live for the Lord; and if we die, we die for the Lord. Whether, therefore, we live or die, we belong to the Lord. This is why Christ died and came to life again, to establish his lordship over dead and living.[3]

We meditate in order to enter into the meaning of those words.

3. Rom. 14:7

The Spirit of Lent

On rereading Paul's first letter to the Thessalonians, which is one of the oldest pieces of Christian writing we have, I was struck once more by the challenge of finding expressions for the ineffable. The great problem for us as Christians is that we use a vocabulary that, just like a currency, can become devalued. We trip off the phrases from our lips – faith, hope, charity – without really understanding the depth of meaning that is involved. The real meaning of faith is vital for a clear understanding of meditation. There is an enormous need for us as persons and as Christians to really develop a faith dimension in our lives if we are to become fully human, fully real, fully rooted in the gift of our own being. And, as I have suggested before, the way of prayer is a way that calls each of us to deepen this faith dimension by deepening our faith in what is.

Consider these words of St Paul writing to the Thessalonians:

> We call to mind, before our God and Father, how your faith has shown itself in action, your love in labour and your hope of our Lord Jesus Christ in fortitude.[1]

Christian hope is above all a supreme confidence that comes to us once we begin to suspect the limitless dimension to the glory of Christ, his splendour and wonder – the words that St Paul constantly uses to express the ineffable. As I have often suggested to you, faith must be a personal response. Each one of us must accept the responsibility to tread this way ourselves and that is what our daily commitment to meditation is about.

So it is with hope. It is a supreme confidence that comes

1. 1 Thess. 1:3

from our conviction that total goodness, complete love, is to be found in our own hearts. So often we can become discouraged. So often we think of ourselves as unworthy, but in the experience of prayer we must not think of ourselves at all. We must not think of our own unworthiness, but what we must *know*, and know with utter clarity, is that the life of God is poured out into our hearts. Just reflect for a moment what an influence for good we could be, as a small meditation group meeting weekly and within the Church as a whole, if each of us could realize our own goodness and if we could realize what the Lord Jesus has achieved for us personally. That is the task of meditation and that is the special task of Lent. Lent is not a time for self-important beating of our breasts and lamenting over our sinfulness. Lent is a time to prepare for the glory of Christ, the glory of Easter, the Paschal glory. We do so, not by concentrating on our own sinfulness, but by forgetting ourselves and by opening our hearts to the Lord Christ.

Our daily meditation is an entry into the supreme conviction that God has revealed himself in Jesus and that Jesus reveals himself to us in our hearts. If only we will pay attention, if only we will be silent, if only we will be simple, humble, obedient. In order to learn that obedience, simplicity and humility, we say our word. Our hope is rooted in the supreme goodness of God. And the hope is made personally real in the supreme goodness he has given to each one of us in Jesus. Listen to how St Paul goes on:

> We are certain, brothers beloved by God, that he has chosen you and that when we brought you the Gospel we brought it, not in mere words, but in the power of the Holy Spirit, and with strong conviction, as you know well.[2]

These words point up the need that our contemporaries have. It is a need for men and women who are not religious bigots, not intolerant of other religious men and women, but who are strong with the power of the Spirit and who know that it is a universal spirit of love. We need Christian people who realize

2. 1 Thess. 1:4

that we have nothing whatever to fear from the Buddhist tradition or the Hindu tradition or any tradition that is truly spiritual. We have only to learn to see one another in the light of Christ. But that we can only do if we allow his light to burn, not just brightly but brilliantly, in our own hearts by standing back, getting out of the way, so that the light of love, compassion and forgiveness may become supreme in our own spirit.

St Paul goes on to say:

And you, in your turn, followed the example set by us and by the Lord; the welcome you gave the message meant great suffering for you, yet you rejoiced in the Holy Spirit.[3]

Meditation is a time of profound joy. It is the peace beyond all understanding, beyond all words, concepts or analysis. Let me remind you again what is involved.

Firstly, a daily commitment and a commitment that goes totally beyond what we feel. We do not meditate when we feel like it or not meditate when we do not feel like it. We accept the discipline of the daily meditation and the daily return to it. Then we accept the discipline of the word of the mantra, the recitation of it from beginning to end. And all because of the glory of God revealed in Jesus. All because of the supreme conviction that Jesus is Lord and that we are able to say that he is Lord because he has given us the Holy Spirit.

3. 1 Thess. 1:6

The Meaning of Silence

There is a great feeling among our contemporaries, I think, of the need, perhaps even the extremely urgent need, to recover the spiritual dimension in our lives. There is a feeling that unless we do recover that spiritual dimension we are going to lose our grip on life altogether. In meeting that feeling we must be perfectly clear that a commitment to spiritual values is by no means a rejection of the ordinary things of life. Indeed the exact opposite is true. Commitment to the spiritual reality is simply commitment to reality and it is the way to really appreciate the wonder of all life. It is the way to come to understand the extraordinary fact of the mystery of life itself, the inner hidden secret of life that gives it its real excitement. Entering on the spiritual path is coming to appreciate our life as a voyage of discovery. It is certainly my experience that, if you set out on the path of meditation with this commitment to enter deeply into your own interior hidden life, then every day for you will become a revelation of new dimensions to that life and a deeper understanding of it.

Now to tread the spiritual path we must learn to be silent. What is required of us is a journey into profound silence. Part of the problem of the weakening of religion in our times is that religion uses words for its prayers and rituals, but those words have to be charged with meaning and they must be charged with sufficient meaning to move our hearts, to set us out in new directions and to change our lives. They can only be charged with this degree of meaning if they spring from spirit, and spirit requires silence. We all need to use words, but to use them with power we all need to be silent. We all need religion, we all need the Spirit. Meditation is the way to silence because it is the way *of* silence. It is the way of the mantra, the word that leads us to such a silence that it ultimately charges all words with meaning. Now we don't need to be too abstract about this. We all know that we can often come to know another person most profoundly in silence. To be silent with another person is a deep expression of trust and confidence and it is only when we are unconfident that we feel compelled to talk. To be silent with another person is truly to *be* with that other person. Nothing is so powerful in building mutual confidence between people than a silence which is easeful and creative. Nothing reveals inauthenticity more dramatically than silence that is not creative but fearful.

I think what all of us have to learn is that we do not have to create silence. The silence is there within us. What we have to do is to enter into it, to become silent, to become the silence. The purpose of meditation and the challenge of meditation is to allow ourselves to become silent enough to allow this interior silence to emerge. Silence is the language of the Spirit.

These words of St Paul writing to the Ephesians, are charged with the power of silence:

> With this in mind, then, I kneel in prayer to the Father, from whom every family in heaven and on earth takes its name, that out of the treasures of his glory he may grant you strength and power through his Spirit in your inner being, that through faith Christ may dwell in your hearts in love.[1]

The words we use in trying to communicate the Christian message in the Christian experience have to be charged with strength and power, but they can only be charged with strength and power if they spring from the silence of the Spirit in our inner being. Learning to say your mantra, leaving behind all other words, ideas, imaginations and fantasies, is learning to enter into the presence of the Spirit who dwells in your inner heart, who dwells there in love. The Spirit of God dwells in our hearts in silence, and it is in humility and in faith that we must enter into that silent presence. St Paul ends that passage in Ephesians with the words, 'So may you attain to fullness of being, the fullness of God himself'. That is our destiny.

1. Eph. 3:14–16

The Life Source

It is important to learn to see meditation as a way of growth, a way of deepening our own commitment to life, and so as a way leading to our own maturity. To see this, it is a most important priority for every one of us to allow our spirit two things: first, the deepest possible contact with the Life Source and then, as a result of that contact, to allow our spirit space within which to expand. Now when we listen to that as a theory it sounds like just so many words. What does it mean for us when we say that a high priority in every life that would be truly human should be this contact with the Life Source?

Every great spiritual tradition has known that in profound stillness the human spirit begins to be aware of its own Source. In the Hindu tradition, for example, the Upanishads speak of the spirit of the One who created the universe as dwelling in our heart. The same spirit is described as the One who in silence is loving to all. In our own Christian tradition Jesus tells us of the Spirit who dwells in our heart and of the Spirit as the Spirit of love. This interior contact with the Life Source is vital for us, because without it we can hardly begin to suspect the potential that our life has for us. The potential is that we should grow, that we should mature, that we should come to fullness of life, fullness of love, fullness of wisdom. The knowledge of that potential is of supreme importance for each of us. In other words, what each of us has to do and what each of us is invited to do is to begin to understand the mystery of our own being as the mystery of life itself.

In the vision proclaimed by Jesus each one of us is invited to understand the sacredness of our own being and life. That is why the second priority is of such great importance: namely, that we should allow our spirit the space within which to expand. In the tradition of meditation this space for expansion of spirit is to be found in silence, and meditation is both a *way* of silence and a *commitment* to silence which grows in every part of our lives. It becomes a silence that we can only describe as the infinite silence of God, the eternal silence. And, as I am sure you will find from your own experience, it is in this silence that we begin to find the humility, the compassion, the understanding that we need for our expansion of spirit. Thoughtful men and women everywhere in the world today are beginning to see that spiritual growth, spiritual awareness, is the highest priority for our time. But the question is – how do we do it? How do we enter on this path?

That is where the tradition of meditation is of supreme importance for us, as a tradition of spiritual commitment by men and women down through the ages and yet a tradition available for you and for me. The only thing that is necessary is that we enter into it by beginning the practice. The practice is very simple and very obvious. We have to put time by, we have to spend some time each morning and each evening of our life to make ourselves available for this work of making contact with the Source of all life and for the work of making space available in our lives for the expansion of spirit. The deepening of faith and the actual practice of meditation are both very simple. Simply take your word, your mantra, and repeat it.

That simplicity is one of the great problems for men and women of our time. We are so used to complexity that the simplicity of meditation, just being content to say your word, to sound your word in your heart, is a major challenge. That is why, when we meditate together or alone, each of us must try to say our word as faithfully as possible, as continually as possible.

The word I recommend you to say, the Aramaic word *maranatha*, should be said without moving your lips, that is, said interiorly in your heart, and you should continue to sound it from the beginning to the end of your time of meditation. Meditation is a process of growing, of growing more spiritually aware and, like all processes of growth it has its own speed, its own pace. It is an organic process. You have as it were to root the mantra in your heart. Jesus so often spoke of the Word of the Gospel taking root in the hearts of men and women and he tells us it has to fall into receptive soil. In other words, the whole of your being has to be involved in this process. You sound the mantra and by your fidelity in returning to it day after day, you root it in your heart and once rooted, it flourishes. Indeed it flowers. And the flower of meditation is peace, a profound peace. It is a peace that arises from harmony, from the dynamic harmony that you encounter when you make contact with the ground of your being, because what you discover is that the mantra is rooted in your heart, the centre of your being, and your being is rooted in God, the centre of all being.

The way of meditation is a way of great simplicity, and so you must take it a day at a time. You don't demand results. You don't look for progress. You simply repeat your mantra every morning and every evening for the entire time of your meditation, and *in the process itself*, which is a process of forgetting yourself, of taking the searchlight of consciousness off yourself, you find yourself in God. Finding yourself in God, you come to an understanding which is the understanding of the *Is*-ness of life. You come to see that your life is a gift, that you offer it back to God and the gift that was a finite gift when it was given to you becomes in the offering back an infinite gift.

Reflect on this in the light of these words from the letter to the Hebrews:

> The kingdom we are given is unshakable; let us therefore give thanks to God, and so worship him as he would be worshipped, with reverence and awe.[1]

The awesomeness of God's closeness to us leads us into profound reverence. We have only to learn to be still, to be silent.

1. Heb. 12:28

The Reality of Faith

This is a Christian understanding of the real nature of faith from the letter to the Hebrews:

> And what is faith? Faith gives substance to our hopes, and makes us certain of realities we do not see. It is for their faith that the men of old stand on record. By faith we perceive that the universe was fashioned by the word of God, so that the visible came forth from the invisible.[1]

The great problem that Christians face in this moment in history is that so many of the words we use to express our belief have failed us. They no longer have power to move our hearts, to change our lives. One of the key words is the word 'faith'. And I think that meditation is of supreme importance for us because it takes us into the experience of faith. Faith is simply openness to, and commitment to, the spiritual reality which is beyond ourselves and yet in which we have our being. St Peter, writing to the early Christians, advised them, 'Hold the Lord Christ in reverence in your hearts,' and the Pauline authors of the letter to the Hebrews tell us that by faith we go beyond what is visible to the invisible, the spiritual reality. Both these insights are rooted in the experience of prayer.

That is why the discipline of our daily commitment to meditation is of such importance. As you know, when you start to meditate and to build prayer into your life, it can be 'kinda fun' to follow up our first burst of spiritual enthusiasm. But when you have to return to your sitting, day by day, and learn to sit in deepening silence and openness, then you soon discover

1. Heb. 11:1–3

that this calls for more and more love on your part, not just enthusiasm. People seeing you will say, 'What are you doing, sitting in silence, doing nothing?' Almost all the values of our society militate against that act of faith whereby you sit down and you close your eyes to the visible and open them to the invisible reality. Later on in the letter to the Hebrews the authors say:

> We must . . . run with resolution the race for which we are entered, our eyes fixed on Jesus, on whom faith depends from start to finish.[2]

That is what faith is about. It is opening our eyes to the larger reality that is revealed in Jesus who reveals to us the Father. Our eyes are taken off ourselves. When we meditate we are not concerned with ourselves, with our own perfection or our own wisdom or even our own happiness. Our eyes are fixed on Jesus and we receive from him everything, literally everything, we need to run the race and everything that we need to make light of the difficulties we have, whatever they are. Jesus – who, for the sake of the joy that lay ahead of him, endured the cross, making light of its disgrace, and has now taken his seat at the right hand of the throne of God.

Meditation does make us 'light of heart', because we know that there is only one thing essential to life and that is that we ourselves are fully open to and fully in harmony with the author of life, the Word through whom we have our being, the incarnate Son of God, our Lord Jesus. Our faith is faith in what the synoptic gospels call 'the Kingdom of God' and the Kingdom of God is simply God's power enthroned in our hearts. This is what makes us light of heart and it is what Christian joy is about.

That power of God is rooted in our heart unshakably. Nothing, no powers, no dominations, no trials can loosen that rootedness of faith. The Kingdom we are given is unshakable. As Christians we have to be able to communicate that Kingdom and that faith. But we can only do so if the reality of that

2. Heb. 12:1–2

Kingdom is not just known to us but embedded in the bedrock of our being. As you know, to meditate is to learn to be profoundly still and profoundly attentive to the spiritual reality. In meditating we learn to distinguish between what is passing away and what endures. We learn to distinguish between time and eternity; and the marvellously liberating experience of prayer is to be liberated from time, to be so profoundly inserted into the present moment of the Kingdom that we glimpse the eternal *now* of God.

> The kingdom we are given is unshakable; let us, therefore, give thanks to God, and so worship him as he would be worshipped, with reverence and awe; for our God is a devouring fire.[3]

Again the authors of the letter to the Hebrews wonderfully proclaim what the Christian invitation is about: to worship, which means to bow and to bend low in spirit before the eternal, the spiritual, the reality that is God. All of us need to find and experience that reverence and that awe, deep in our own heart, deep in our own spirit. The simple exercise of our repeated word brings us to that simplicity, the necessary poverty of spirit. The author of *The Cloud of Unknowing* speaks of meditation as the exercise that loosens the root of sin within us. Saying your word, meditating every morning and every evening, loosens the root of the ego within you, and all of us need that root to be loosened so that we may be rooted and founded in Christ.

Listen again to the letter to the Hebrews:

> Remember where you stand: not before the palpable, blazing fire of Sinai. . . . you stand before Mount Zion and the city of the living God, . . . and Jesus, the mediator of a new covenant.[4]

To prepare to meditate simply listen to this call to faith from the letter to the Hebrews, and let us by our profound stillness

3. Heb. 12:28–9   4. Heb. 12:18, 22, 24

and silence, be led into that reverence and awe, led to know that we are in the presence of the Lord Jesus, the mediator of the New Covenant, the Covenant of Love.

The Wholeness of God

In these talks we are always starting again. It is not that in each talk anything new is said, but our aim in each talk is to come, surely and gradually, nearer the centre of the mystery. Meditation is always a return to our beginning, which is our centre and our source. Each time we sit down to meditate, every morning and every evening, our aim is to clear the ground so that the energy at the centre may radiate freely and penetrate universally. We have only one ultimate hazard, and that hazard is distraction.

As we all know from our own sad experience we are so easily distracted. God's love is given to each of us freely and generously and universally. God's love flows in our hearts in a mighty stream. But, like Martha in the gospel story, we are all of us so busy about so many things. We have to learn, and it is absolutely necessary that we do learn it, that only one thing is necessary, because only one thing *is*. All of us must therefore address our own lack of discipline. We must bring our restless wandering minds to stillness. It is one of the first great lessons in humility we learn, when we realize that we come to wisdom and stillness, and we pass beyond distraction, only through the gift of God. His prayer is his gift to us and all we have to do is to dispose ourselves, and this we can do by becoming silent. Silence is the essential human response to the mystery of God, to the infinity of God. We learn to be silent by being content to say our mantra in humble fidelity.

It is as though the mystery of God is a wonderful multi-faceted diamond. When we talk or think about God it is as though we are responding to one or another of his facets, but when we are silent – which is to say, in his presence – we respond to the mystery which we call God *as a whole* and do

83

so omni-dimensionally. The wonder of it is that it is the whole of us that responds to the entirety of the mystery of God. It is not just our intellect, not just our emotions, not just the 'religious' side of us or the 'secular' side of us. Everything that we are responds to everything that he is, in absolute harmony, in absolute love. That is what the experience of Christian prayer is. A wholeness. The essence of the wholeness is to be found in our union with him who is One.

How is this possible? It is possible through the Incarnate Reality which is Jesus. God is fully revealed in Jesus, fully present in Jesus. The love of Jesus has made us one with him. By becoming open through silence to his reality we become open in wonder to the reality of God. That is why the way of prayer is a way of ever deeper, ever more generous silence. It is not enough just to think about silence or to talk about silence – we must embrace it! To learn this silence, to be open to the gift of it, we must learn to say our mantra. Our regular times of meditation immerse us in this silence and we emerge from the silence refreshed, renewed and re-baptized in the power of the Spirit. As I have so often said to you before, what each of us discovers in our prayer is that simply to *be* in his presence is all sufficing. In that presence we are healed. In that presence we find the courage to live our lives through him, with him, in him and for him. Once we begin to be open to this power, everything in our lives is charged with meaning. The meaning comes out of the silence. All our talking, all our living, all our loving find meaning from this silence and flow back into it.

People often ask,'What is the experience of prayer like? What is it really like?' By that they mean, 'What happens?' What is it like? It is like silence. And what happens? In the silence – peace. In the silence – presence. And deeper silence. The way into that silence requires great patience, great fidelity and it requires in our tradition of meditation that we learn to say our mantra. As John Cassian said, the mantra contains all the human mind can express and all the human heart can feel. That one little word conveys and leads us into the silence which is the silence of creative energy. How long this takes us is of no concern to us. 'To the Lord a thousand years are as a day.' The only thing that matters is that we are on the way and that means the simplicity of our daily meditations, every morning, every evening.

The wonder of the way is caught in these words of St Paul writing to the Romans:

> Therefore, my brothers, I implore you by God's mercy to offer your very selves to him: a living sacrifice, dedicated and fit for his acceptance, the worship offered by mind and heart. Adapt yourselves no longer to the pattern of this present world, but let your minds be remade and your whole nature thus transformed. Then you will be able to discern the will of God, and to know what is good, acceptable, and perfect.[1]

1. Rom. 12:1–2

Being Yourself

The two big questions about meditation we have to consider are, firstly – Why should we meditate? and secondly – How do you meditate? In our Introductory Night talks to our groups what we try to look at is not so much – 'Why should you meditate?' but the question – 'How do you meditate?' If you genuinely look at the first question, it is my personal conviction that meditation can add a dimension of incredible richness to your life. I wish that I had the persuasive powers or the eloquence to convince everyone that I meet of the importance of meditating.

The importance of it is that you can be yourself. When you are meditating you do not have to apologize for being, you do not have to try to make yourself acceptable to anyone else, you do not have to play any role. One of the roles you have to beware of playing is any sort of spiritual role ('I am now getting into my holy act'). You just sit still and it is in that stillness that you gain the wisdom to see that you can only be yourself, you can only become yourself who is the person you are created to be, if you are willing to lose yourself. The truth that you can discover from your own experience is this – that any one of us can only find ourselves in the other. No amount of self-analysis or self-examination, will ever reveal to you who you are. But if you can take the focus of your attention off yourself and project it forward then you will discover the other and in discovering *your other*, you will discover *your self*.

The *other* is the Ground of All Being, the other we call God, Supreme Wisdom, Supreme Being, Supreme Love. The name is not important. Indeed, in meditation and in the silence of it, the complete silence of it, we go beyond all names, beyond all words, to the Reality.

But now I want to repeat *how* we meditate. It is necessary to repeat this over and over again just because meditating is so simple. For us, as self-consciously complex Westerners, it is difficult to believe and to accept that anything so simple could be so powerful. So once again, to meditate, what you have to learn to do is to sit still and recite, interiorly, in your heart, in your mind, a word or phrase. The word I have recommended you to recite is the Aramaic word *maranatha* to be recited as four equally-stressed syllables 'Ma-ra-na-tha'. That is all there is to meditating. I first learnt to meditate some thirty years or so ago, and my teacher used to say to me – in answer to whatever the question I put to him about meditation – 'Say your mantra, say your word'. The longer I have meditated over the years, the more I have realized the absolute wisdom of what he taught me. If you can learn just to say your word and keep saying it, keep repeating it throughout the twenty or twenty-five minutes or half-an-hour of your meditation, keep repeating it from the beginning to the end, you will eventually be unhooked from your ideas, your concepts, your words, your thoughts, all that amalgam of distraction that is going on in your mind most of the time, and you will come, with patience and with fidelity, to clarity of consciousness.

Now let's look at some practical questions. What should you do if, when you sit down to meditate you feel very nervous or you begin to see colours or hear noises or whatever? – all of these probably symptoms of tension. A very simple relaxation exercise is to lie on the flat of your back, spend a couple of moments allowing the floor to take the weight of your body and then breathe in very deeply into the diaphragm. Don't move the chest, but hold the breath in your diaphragm for about five or seven seconds or so and then exhale through the mouth. Do that about ten times, then sit up and then, or later, meditate. You will find that it is a very relaxing exercise and, to begin with, it might be very useful for you to precede your meditation with a little relaxing exercise of that kind. Because for most of the day we are fairly tense. We are having to deal with driving through traffic or dealing with our job or family problems, and this all leaves us fairly tense. But as you progress in your meditation, the meditation times themselves will bring you to a much deeper relaxation and you will probably be able to come straight from your work or other activity into your meditation and become quite relaxed straight away.

The other point to notice when you are beginning is that whatever phenomena present themselves to you – whether you see colours or hear sounds or see visions, whatever it is – take it as the general principle that it is all utterly unimportant. It has no real significance of any kind, except perhaps that you may need to be a bit more relaxed before you start. One of the things you have to learn in approaching your meditation is to approach it by not expecting anything. A lot of us in the West, when we begin meditating hope it will bring us to see visions or to understand life with deeper insight, teach us wisdom or knowledge. But you must come to it absolutely generous and absolutely poor in spirit, that is, without demands or any sort of expectations other than this – a conviction that you will come to in the meditation itself – that this is what we were created for. This is what everyone reading this book was created for – to be, and to be in relationship with our Creator.

That is the fundamental relationship of our existence – creature and Creator. In meditating you enter into the harmony of that relationship. You put yourself into harmony with the Creator and so one of the fruits of meditation is that the harmony which you discover in yourself you also begin to discover everywhere. So, the truly spiritual man or woman is someone who is in harmony with everyone they meet. You meet others not on the basis of competition or of projecting any image to them of who you might be or would like to be or think you ought to be. But you begin to meet everyone as you are, the person you are, comfortable, accepting of your own being. And you accept it because, in the silence of your meditation, you come to the knowledge that you are accepted. It is not just that you are acceptable because you have done all the right things. What you discover as you begin to explore that basic relationship of creature–Creator is that you are accepted. In the Christian vision of meditation you discover something even more. You discover in the silence that you are loved, that you are lovable. It is the discovery that everyone must make in their lives if they are going to become fully themselves, fully human.

In the vision proclaimed by Jesus you begin to know what St John meant when he said, 'God is love'. The extraordinary thing is (and this is again what I personally would like to be able to convey, to communicate to everyone I meet) that that love is to be found in your own heart. Each of you, if only you can come to this silence, will find it. If only you can come to the space within yourselves where you can discover that you can breathe this pure air of love.

Going back to this first question, 'Why should you meditate?', this is really why we meditate. To come to what perhaps we can describe best as a pure liberty of spirit. In meditation you are utterly un-constrained. You are not in any way enslaved to any image or idea, because you are beyond all images and ideas and you are in that state where you have the perfect liberty to be yourself. You have that liberty because you are one with the One who is. If you want to ask yourself when you put this book down, 'What is meditation really about?' just say to yourself, 'It is about being. It is about *is*-ness. He is. I am.' You can say either of those, but ultimately the experience of meditation is concerned with *being*.

Now let me just remind you again. We meditate at first for about twenty-five minutes and I should repeat the importance of being as still as you can. It is not a hard task. If you feel that you really must move, then don't feel that you will ruin everything by moving. But learn in time to sit as still as you possibly can because meditation is about a unity of body and spirit and a stillness of body and spirit. So when you start, take a moment to get really comfortable in your sitting posture and then begin to say your mantra. Don't think about anything. Don't think, 'Why am I doing this? Am I getting anything out of this?' Don't encourage any thoughts. Just say the word and listen to the word. My heartfelt advice to you is that if you do want to learn to meditate it is necessary to meditate every day in your life for a minimum of twenty minutes in the morning and twenty minutes in the evening. The ideal time is probably about half an hour. If you find that too long to begin with, start with twenty and gradually increase it to thirty minutes.

The ideal time to meditate is before your breakfast and before your evening meal. The place should be quiet and if possible always the same place.

Turn from your own thoughts now by attending to this reading from St Paul's letter to the Colossians. He is speaking about what Jesus will do for each of us if we are truly open to him:

> May he strengthen you, in his glorious might, with ample power to meet whatever comes with fortitude, patience and joy; and to give thanks to the Father who has made you fit to share the heritage of God's people in the realm of light.[1]

Meditation is about enlightenment because it is about coming into the light of God. That is the basic relationship, Creator and creature. And the Creator gives each of us the light to be ourselves.

1. Col. 1:11–12

Space to Be

St Paul writes this to the Thessalonians:

> We are bound to thank God always for you, brothers beloved
> by the Lord, because from the beginning of time God chose
> you to find salvation in the Spirit that consecrates you, and
> in the truth that you believe.[1]

I think it is a major concern of everyone to come to know
themselves, to understand themselves, and one of the great
ways put forward for this in our own society is experience.
People are encouraged to experiment with their experience.
But I think experience is only useful and only instructive for
us if we are able to evaluate it adequately. So often, as we all
know from our past, we have the experience but we missed the
meaning.

Our monastic tradition tells us that, if we want to understand
ourselves and to know who we are, then we have to make
contact with our own centre. We have to make contact with
the Ground of our being where this centre is, and unless that
process is underway all our experience will leave us in the
shallows. More and more people in our society are coming to
understand that both our personal problems and the problems
that we face as a society are basically spiritual ones. What more
and more of us are understanding in this world is that the
human spirit cannot find fulfilment in mere material success or
material prosperity. It isn't that material success or prosperity
are bad in themselves but they are simply not adequate as a
final, ultimate answer to the human situation.

1. 2 Thess. 2:13

So many men and women are discovering that their spirit is stifled as a result of the materialism in which we live, and much of the frustration in our time is due to the feeling that we were created for something better than this, something more serious than just a day-to-day survival. To know ourselves, to understand ourselves and to be able to start solving our problems, to get ourselves and our problems into perspective, we simply must make contact with our spirit. All self-understanding arises from understanding ourselves as spiritual beings, and it is only contact with the universal Holy Spirit that can give us the depth and the breadth to understand our own experience. The way to this is not difficult. It is very simple. But it does require serious commitment and serious involvement in our own existence.

The wonderful revelation that is there for all of us to discover, if only we will set out on the path with discipline, is that our spirit is rooted in God and that each of us has an eternal destiny and an eternal significance and importance. That is a primary discovery for each of us to make, that the nature we possess has this infinite potential for development and that development can only come if we undertake this pilgrimage to our own centre. Our centre is our own heart because it is only there, in the depths of our own being, that we can discover ourselves rooted in God. Meditation is just this way of making contact with our own spirit and in that contact finding the way of integration, of finding everything in our experience coming into harmony, everything in our experience judged and aligned on God.

The way of meditation is very simple. All each of us has to do is to be as still as possible in body and in spirit. The stillness of body we achieve by sitting still. So each time you begin to meditate take a couple of moments to assume a comfortable posture. The only essential rule is to have your spine as upright as possible. Then the way to the stillness of spirit that we have in our monastic tradition is to learn to say silently, in the depth of our spirit, a word or a short phrase. The art of meditation is simply learning to repeat that word over and over again – the word I have recommended you to use is the Aramaic word, *maranatha*. Don't move your lips, but recite it interiorly. What is important and you must understand from the beginning, is to recite your word from the beginning to the end of your time of meditation. Learning to meditate is learning to let go of your thoughts, ideas and imagination and to rest in the depths of your own being. Always remember that. Don't think, don't use any words other than your one word, don't imagine anything. Just sound, say the word in the depths of your spirit and listen to it. Concentrate upon it with all your attention.

Why is this so powerful? Basically, because it gives us the space that our spirit needs to breathe. It gives each of us the space to be ourselves. When you are meditating you don't need to apologize for yourself and you don't need to justify yourself. All you need to do is to *be* yourself, to accept from the hands of God the gift of your own being, and in that acceptance of yourself and your creation you come into harmony with the Creator, with *the* Spirit. Meditation is about our spirit coming totally into harmony with the Spirit of God. But if you want to learn to meditate and to live your life from the depth of your being, then you must build this into your every day and make a space in your life every morning and every evening. The minimum time is about twenty minutes, the optimum time about thirty minutes. Once you do learn that discipline you will begin to live your life in harmony, harmony within yourself, because everything in your life will come into harmony with God, and harmony with all creation, because you will have found your place, your place in creation. The astonishing thing about the Christian revelation is that your place is nothing less than to be rooted and founded in God.

From the pilgrimage of meditation we hear St Paul with new ears:

> We are bound to thank God always for you, brothers beloved by the Lord, because from the beginning of time God chose you to find salvation in the Spirit that consecrates you, and in the truth that you believe. It was for this that he called you through the gospel we brought, so that you might possess for your own the splendour of our Lord Jesus Christ.[2]

2. 2 Thess. 2:13–14

That is what the path of meditation is about. To come into full harmony, to full union with the Spirit of Jesus who dwells in our hearts.

The One Centre

It is always important to try to put before ourselves a general idea of what meditation is about. For those of you who have been meditating for a while this will be like a little revision. For those who are about to start it can serve as an introduction.

Basically, meditation is a way of coming to your own centre, the foundation of your own being, and remaining there – still, silent, attentive. Meditation is in essence a way of learning to become awake, fully alive and yet still. It is the stillness of meditation that leads you forward to that state of wakefulness and the sense of being completely alive that dawns in you because you are in harmony with yourself and, gradually, in harmony with the whole of creation. The experience of meditation puts you in resonance with all life. But the way to that resonance, the way to that wakefulness is silence and stillness.

This is quite a challenge for people of our time, because most of us have very little experience of silence, and silence can be terribly threatening to people in the transistorized culture that we live in. You have to get used to that silence. That is why the way of meditation is a way of learning to say the word interiorly, in your heart. The purpose of repeating the word is to launch you into the silence. So, lay aside all kinds of materialistic ideas about how long this will take. It might take twenty years. But that doesn't matter at all. It might take twenty minutes. That doesn't matter either. The only important thing if you want to re-establish contact with your centre is to be on the way. The wonderful thing we discover when we do get underway is that there is only one centre, that that centre is everywhere and that meditation is the way of being linked to it in our own centre. Because we are then rooted in ourselves we find our place in the universe and so we find the centre of the universe. We find God.

The truly spiritual man or woman is the person who is so rooted in themselves that they are able to be in harmony with anyone and everyone. The whole purpose of the spiritual journey is to enter into a profound harmony with yourself, your neighbour, the universe and with God. Let me remind you again. The way to do this, the way of meditation is a way of utter simplicity. You have to learn to say your word, 'Maranatha'. It is difficult, just because this is not the conventional wisdom. Most people in our society think that wisdom is about growing in complexity and the more abstruse and rarefied the ideas that you can examine and master, the wiser you will become. If you say to someone, 'I am going just to sit down every morning and every evening and I am going to learn to say this word,' many people will say to you, 'Well you must be a fool. Surely life is too precious, and time too precious for you to waste time, for half an hour in the morning and half an hour in the evening, just saying a word like this. Weren't you given your mind for something more worthy, something better than that?'

So it takes a good deal of courage for each of us, as men and women of the twentieth century, actually to sit down and to meditate, every morning and every evening. But that is what is required. If you want to learn to meditate, you must try to make that time available each morning and each evening, and you must learn the discipline and be prepared for it as a real discipline. It is a discipline that will bring you to great stability, to great unity, to great harmony. The discipline is the discipline of saying the word.

A friend of mine recently sent me a cartoon from the *New Yorker*. It was of two Buddhist-like monks sitting in a meditation posture and one was saying under his breath to the one sitting beside him, 'What do you mean what happens next? This is it.' That is how a lot of people in our society see meditation. Another cartoon someone sent me a little while ago was a picture of a long-haired youth sitting in a meditation posture and his father, evidently an executive of some sort, was talking to some friends of his saying, 'It is absolutely marvellous, you know. Before he took up this meditation, he just sat around all day doing nothing.' That would give you an idea, if you just consider the humour of the *New Yorker*, as to how people in our society view meditation.

We ourselves should approach it, I think, with a certain humour too and not get too solemn about it. But that is the deal. That is what is required. If you want to learn to meditate, you must learn to sit still and to say your word from beginning to end. Now what you will find, if you can persevere, is that after a little while of saying the word you will feel a certain peacefulness and relaxation and you will be tempted to say to yourself, 'This is rather good. I'd like just to experience this now and to know what I am feeling now, I'll give up saying the word. I'll just go with the experience.' That is the high road to disaster. You meditate not to experience the experience. You meditate to enter into the experience. Meditation is a coming to consciousness and a going beyond self-reflective consciousness. Meditation is learning to look out beyond yourself, breaking out of the closed system of self-consciousness, that prison of the ego, and we do so by that discipline of saying the word. When you are saying the word you are not thinking your own thoughts. You are not analysing what is happening to you. You are letting go. Meditation, in the Christian vision of it, is simply launching out into the infinity of God through the Spirit who dwells in our hearts. It is a letting go, a launching out into the deep. And people, in all ages throughout history, have found that it requires an act of faith to leave yourself behind.

So, do not complicate your meditation. In my humble opinion, the less you read about meditation the better. The less you talk about meditation, the better. The real thing is to meditate. The simple rule to remember is this – find a quiet place in your home or wherever you are at the time. Sit down and sit upright. Don't bother when you begin with too much of technique. It is not necessary to sit in the lotus position. It may be very helpful if you can. It might be worth learning. But sit upright. The essential rule of posture is that your spine is as upright as possible. Breathing – the simple rule is breathe. Do not get too het up about whether you should breathe in or breathe out. Do both! Then, the rule that is the most important of all – say your mantra, say your word. And that is the art of meditation, to learn to say it from the beginning to the end.

Simple Enjoyment of the Truth

St Thomas Aquinas says that 'contemplation consists in the simple enjoyment of the truth'. Simple enjoyment! Now it is true that thinking, analysing, comparing and contrasting, all have their place in all the various disciplines, including theology. But contemplation, as St Thomas calls it, meditation as we would call it, is not the time for activity, for the activity of thinking, analysing, comparing or contrasting. Meditation is the time for being. Simple enjoyment. And the simplicity that St Thomas speaks of is oneness, union.

The challenge to us as men and women of the twentieth century is that we live in an age that stresses activity, and it seems that if we are to come to terms with our problems and difficulties then surely we must *do* something about it. I was talking to a man yesterday who met someone in a hotel and they started to talk about the problems of life. The man he was talking to said, 'You know you could solve all this if only you would follow a course that I am going to.' And my friend said to him, 'How long will it take?' The fellow thought for a moment and he said, 'About ten days'. And then he described the course, all the various techniques that are required for activating personal fulfilment and so forth. Our society is full of this sort of thing – how to win friends and influence people. All these courses are full of exercises, procedures, questionnaires to be filled out, profiles to be elaborated and so forth. Many of them even consist of the technique of exhausting the participants, keeping them short of food, announcing that there will be a food-break shortly which never comes. (Indeed, the course that was described to my friend went on until four o'clock in the morning!)

So all these courses (and they are rife in our society) have a lot of content in them, much input and they demand intense activity. No doubt there is a place for some of them. But there is an ancient Islamic story which we should listen to before taking one of these courses. It tells of a man in a town at night looking for his key that he has dropped. He is looking under a street lamp, searching everywhere for the key. A passer-by sees him searching and says, 'What are you looking for?' 'My key,' he said, 'I've dropped it.' And so the passer-by searches too, everywhere. There is not a sign of the key. The passer-by says to him, 'Where did you drop it?' And he said, 'Down the road there about fifty yards.' The passer-by asked, 'Well, why are you looking here?' He said, 'Well, there is more light here.'

Now I think that we are very much like that man looking for our key where there is more light. Everyone in our society, I suppose to some extent, is searching for the key to the mystery of life, through all sorts of techniques and procedures. No doubt, each of them has a certain validity. But the search that we are talking about is beyond all activity. It is not a matter of assimilating more knowledge. It is really a matter of letting go, a running off. In fact, it is not a search, strictly speaking at all. We are not, as it were, looking for God who is lost. We know that he is here, that he is now. We know that he is present in this space, in this time, and the path of meditation we are following is simply to be open to what is, to the *is*-ness of God and to the *is*-ness of our own creation. This openness requires of each of us that we become present to the *now*, the here, and that we pay attention at the core of our being. That is the challenge of Christian meditation. In a way, we have to leave the street lamp that is familiar to us in our own society and we have to go off where there is no such clear light. We have to go into the dark. Learning to say our mantra is just that commitment to finding the light within ourselves.

St Thomas speaks of simple enjoyment of the truth. The mantra is the key to that simplicity. The mantra is indeed a principle of pure simplicity. It is the definitive leaving of complexity behind. Only one word. Childlike faith to say the one word. The truth that St Thomas speaks is the only truth there is. The Truth who is also the Way, the Truth who is also Life.

Meditation is equally simple enjoyment of the Way. Simple enjoyment of life. When we meditate we become as it were reduced to our essential being. In that reduction we become small enough to enter through the eye of the needle. Meditation teaches us humility, and in coming to that smallness, undergoing that reduction, we enter out into life, unlimited life. Apply this to the teaching of St John's Gospel:

The time approaches, indeed it is already here, when those who are real worshippers will worship the Father in spirit and in truth. Such are the worshippers whom the Father wants. God is spirit and those who worship him must worship in spirit and in truth.[1]

Meditation is the way of making full contact with your own spirit, of making full contact with truth. Remember the Way. Say your mantra from the beginning to the end. Meditate every morning and every evening, faithfully, simply and humbly. Contemplation consists in the simple enjoyment of the truth.

1. John 4:23–4

101

The Light of Christ

These words are from the Gospel of John:

> If you dwell within the revelation I have brought, you are
> indeed my disciples; you shall know the truth, and the truth
> will set you free.[1]

Meditation could be described as a way of truth. The Greek
word for truth *aletheia* comes from 'a–lethes' which means
something that is not hidden. So, *aletheia* suggests that the
truth is a revelation for us. It is a revelation of the essential
structure of things. I want to talk a little about meditation as
a *way* of revelation.

As we all know we begin to meditate with all our confusion
around us. We do not even quite understand why we are meditating. I think a lot of us start as very reluctant meditators. We
hear about it and we begin in a half-hearted sort of way. But
gradually a glimmer of light comes. We suspect that there might
be something in it. The darkness is still all around us but there
is just the faintest glimmer of light. When that happens the first
step to take is to start meditating seriously, not with half your
heart but whole-heartedly. That means to put the time aside
for this way of revelation every morning and every evening.
That is the first thing to do. The second step is to begin to
commit yourself (and it takes time because you have to be
patient) to saying your mantra for the entire time of your
meditation. You should not be discouraged if you are a slow
starter. It takes some of us four or five years to come to that
stage. But what you will discover from your own perseverance

1. John 8:31–2

is that saying the mantra is like a very gentle and very gradual dispelling of the dark.

Just imagine for a moment a vast, dark, empty hall. Each time you say your mantra it is like lighting a small weak candle. And I think so often it seems to us that just as we light one, the previous one gets blown out. But very gradually the dawn comes and you begin to realize that the whole hall is flooded with light. The wonder of meditation is that this revelation that the light has conquered the darkness and that Jesus is the light becomes universal in your experience. Everything and everyone is now flooded, illuminated with this light.

This is very different from the pagan conception of things. You may know of the story in *Beowulf* when the banqueters and revellers are in the hall and suddenly a bird flies in through a window, briefly through the hall and out again into the dark. The revellers look at the bird flying in one window and out of the other, and they say, 'This is what human life is like. Out of darkness, a brief moment of revelry and back into the darkness again.' Now in the vision proclaimed by Jesus the under-standing of the human condition is totally different. For us the banqueting hall is the heart, and that is where the darkness is when we begin. But by the discipline of our daily commitment, which is our commitment to the light in spite of our own weakness and in spite of our own half-hearted starts and false starts, we can find in our hearts the light that is also outside our hearts. The marvel of the proclamation of the Gospel by Jesus is that everyone and everything, inner and outer, is enlightened in a universal dawn of grace. This is what the power of the cross is about. This is what the power of the resurrection of Jesus is about. The universal dawn has occurred, and our commitment is to that enlightenment, that truth and that revelation. We have been using the metaphor of the light. What is the light for us who accept the revelation of Jesus?

The light is nothing less than the consciousness of Jesus himself. I do not think it is wrong to say that while we are looking for him we are always looking for the wrong thing because so often as Christians we are looking for an object of knowledge distinct from ourselves, but the truth is that we have already found Christ. We have found him when we realize –

103

that is, when we know fully – that what he has achieved for us is that we see with his vision. We see with his consciousness. We understand with his understanding because his invitation to us is that we should be united with him, one with him. It is not true to say that he is just within us or just beyond us. He is both within us and beyond us, and the enlightenment of Jesus enlightens us and enlightens the whole of creation. The challenge to us, and the great challenge to our belief, is that such an elusive mystery is not beyond our experience. It is not too difficult for us, but we can know it intimately and power-fully only when we forget ourselves. What we have to learn in our meditation is that the loss of self-consciousness enables us to come to full consciousness both with him and in him, with his own self-knowledge.

How do we lose our self-consciousness? It is very simple. It is very practical. The simple tool we use is that we must stop thinking about ourselves. That is why we have to learn to say the mantra. When we learn to say it with our total attention, with an undivided heart, we are on our way to being what Jesus invites us to be, one with him as he is one with the Father. In that oneness we are made free and we have been freed by the revelation of Jesus himself, because what he reveals to us is the glory, the wonder and the love of the Father. In this con-sciousness let us listen to St John again:

> He who sent me is present with me, and has not left me alone; for I always do what is acceptable to him. . . . If you dwell within the revelation I have brought, you are indeed my disciples; you shall know the truth, and the truth will set you free. . . . If then the Son sets you free, you will indeed be free.[2]

2. John 8:29, 31–2, 36

104

The Inner Christ

Who is going to do you wrong if you are devoted to what is good? And yet if you should suffer for your virtues, you may count yourself happy. Have no fear of them; do not be perturbed, but hold the Lord Christ in reverence in your hearts.[1]

'Hold the Lord Christ in reverence . . . in your hearts.' The world in which we live is passing away. As we all know, empires arise. They have great periods of power and then they crumble. The lesson of history is that when they crumble they crumble very quickly. Wisdom in this situation is the ability to identify what endures, to understand what lasts and what is truly important. The early Christian community understood very clearly that each of us possesses and possesses right now, in this life, an eternal principle within us, something in our hearts that endures for all eternity – the Lord Christ. And so we are to 'hold the Lord Christ in reverence in our hearts'.

To live our lives well we don't need to be depressed by the fact that the world is passing away, that civilizations do crumble. Nor do we need to be disturbed by the fact that the world is often a largely chaotic world. As we all know, there is so much confusion. There are so many people who are confused, and all of us know that from time to time in our lives we experience that chaos and confusion in ourselves. But the challenge for each of us, and one that every human person must ultimately face, is to find in the real world, that is, a world that is chaotic and passing away, true peace, adequate order and a harmony that will make sense of all the voices competing

1. 1 Pet. 3:13–15

105

for our attention. Again, the early Christian community saw clearly, because they knew from their own experience, that Jesus himself is the way to order, harmony and peace. They know that he is the way because he leads us into the resonant harmony of the Trinity itself, the order, the supreme order, that is based on the supreme love of the Father, the Son and Holy Spirit.

The way of meditation is not a way of escape. Above all, it is not a way of illusion. We neither try to escape the real world of untidy ends and chaotic beginnings and nor do we try to construct an alternative, illusory reality of our own. What Jesus promises us is that if we do hold him in reverence in our hearts, if we believe in him and believe in the one who sent him, his Father and our Father, then all the chaos and all the confusion in the world can have no ultimate power over us. The stresses, the strains, the challenges, all remain but they are powerless to defeat us when we have founded our lives on the rock who is Christ. This is the real task. This is the real challenge that each of us must face, to enter into the reality that is Christ, the rock on whom we can build our lives with the absolute assurance that he will love us through all our mistakes, through all our changes of heart and mind and through every moment of our lives until the last moment of our life, because he is supreme love.

That is why St Peter tells us of the importance of holding the Lord Christ in reverence in our hearts. Rooted in him we are rooted in the principle of all life, in reality itself and, founded in him, nothing else has ultimate power over us, not even death itself. The challenge is to find our way to him by finding the way to our own heart so that we can hold him in reverence there. The way of meditation is consequently a way of learning to die to illusion, to all unreality, and so it is the way of learning to rise with Christ, to rise beyond ourselves and our limitations to eternal life. It is learning to do this now, today, and not to postpone eternal life to a time when we may get to heaven. The Kingdom of Heaven is among us now and we must be open to it now because, as St Peter says, we must be alive in the Spirit and become fully alive with the life of God. As Christians we must never settle for less. Our Christian life is not just a question of finding a way of getting through our lives. Every word of the New Testament suggests to us that it is of supreme importance that we live our lives in a state of continuous expansion, expansion of heart and expansion of Spirit, growing in love and becoming more firmly rooted in God. Each of us has to understand our potential, that we *are* an expanding universe, and so each of us possesses the potential for an energy-expansion that is not less than infinite.

St Peter tells us in the same letter 'to live an ordered life, founded on prayer' and he tells us 'to keep our love for one another at full strength'. This is the way of meditation – to tap that life source, that source of energy and power so that we can live our lives to the full. And we do so holding the Lord Christ in reverence in our hearts. Listen to St Peter again:

Who is going to do you wrong if you are devoted to what is good? And yet if you should suffer for your virtues, you may count yourselves happy. Have no fear of them: do not be perturbed, but hold the Lord Christ in reverence in your hearts. . . . Why was the Gospel preached to those who are dead? In order that, although in the body they received the sentence common to men, they might in the spirit be alive with the life of God. . . . you must lead an ordered and sober life, given to prayer. Above all, keep your love for one another at full strength, because love cancels innumerable sins.[2]

2. 1 Pet. 3:13–15; 4:6, 7–8

Free to be True

These are words spoken by Jesus and recorded in the Gospel of John:

> If you dwell within the revelation I have brought, you are indeed my disciples; you shall know the truth, and the truth will set you free.[1]

All of us, I think, feel within ourselves the primary necessity to come to grips with the truth. It is a need to find something, some principle in our lives that is absolutely reliable and worthy of our confidence. All of us feel this impulse to somehow or other make contact with rock-like reality. In the Old Testament truth was seen as an attribute of God and it was felt as God's trustworthiness. In him you could have complete confidence because he was true – as the Old Testament expressed it, 'Yahweh will not depart from his word'.

Now this is what the path of meditation is about. When we set out on the path of meditation we set out on the path of truth. 'His word is true.' Of course none of us can be just content with other people's experience of the truth, and so all of us have to come to know the truth from our own experience. If you want to follow this path, you have to commit yourself to meditating every day, to meditating every morning and every evening. The way is simplicity itself. All you have to do is to sit down and say your word, 'Maranatha'. When we meditate alone or in a group each of us has to accept the responsibility of saying the mantra from beginning to end. The saying of the word is itself an experience of liberty. We let go of all our

1. John 8:31–2

immediate concerns – everything that troubles us today, everything that makes us happy today. We turn aside from everything that is passing away in order to be open to absolute and ultimate Truth.

Wisdom teaches us that arriving at the Truth is experiencing the graciousness and loving kindness of God. And in the Christian vision of meditation the whole purpose of meditation is simply to be open to this presence of God in our hearts. People often ask, 'Why should I meditate? Why do *you* meditate?' I think part of the answer is that in the experience of meditation we come to know ourselves as true, as real, not ourselves as acting a role, not ourselves fulfilling other people's expectations of us, but the experience of being who we are. Meditation is important for us because each of us has to learn how to be true, how to be faithful to the truth of our own being. The one who is true is the one who is faithful. And the power of meditation is that in the personal experience of it, in the silence to which our word leads us, we learn to live out of the goodness of God when we have made contact with his goodness in our hearts. God is true, and anyone who discovers their own oneness with God has entered into the fundamental relationship of life, and as a result of this relationship all our relationships are filled with the kindliness and the truth of God. Jesus says, 'The truth will set you free.' The freedom is the freedom to be ourselves and the freedom to let others be themselves. The freedom to love ourselves, to love others and to love God. But that freedom depends upon a total commitment to truth.

People ask, 'How long will this take?' or they say, 'I have been meditating every morning and every evening for six months and I'm not sure if it has made any difference yet.' The answer to that is that it doesn't matter how long it takes. All that matters is that we are truthfully on the way, on the pilgrimage, and that each day – although perhaps only by one centimetre at a time – our commitment to truth and to freedom grows. The growth is often imperceptible, but that does not matter. All that matters is that we are growing, that we have not settled for half and that we have not betrayed the gift of our own being but that we are committed to growth and to maturity.

The opposite of the truth is falsehood or illusion, and meditation is a single-minded, clear-sighted commitment to the truth. It is a commitment to turn away from trying to make our own reality towards living in the light of God and by the light of God. The daily commitment to it, and the powerful gentleness of it as we meditate day by day, is a way of learning to accustom our eyes to seeing what is really before us rather than trying to imagine what is before us and then taking that for reality. What is real? What is truth?

God is real and the reality of God is the truth revealed in Jesus. The greatest part of the Christian proclamation of the Gospel is that Jesus in all his reality is to be found in our own hearts. In his light we see light. And in that light we know ourselves to be free. Now when you begin you have to begin in faith, and you have to continue in faith because the only way of arriving at that light, at the truth and the freedom, is by faith. Every time you sit down to meditate, your faith will be tested and so your faith will be strengthened. The time of meditation, when you say your mantra from beginning to end, might often seem to you to be a complete waste of time, but only remember that Jesus dwells in your heart. He is the revelation of God. Only in God and only from God do we have our reality. Saying the mantra is turning from all illusion, from all imagination, from all falsehood to ultimate Truth. Remind yourself of the way continuously. Sit comfortably, upright and as still as you can. Meditation is a way of total stillness, body and spirit. Then say your word as faithfully as you can.

There is a great power in meditating together. Your pilgrimage will be greatly helped by finding a group to meditate with regularly. We share that faith that is necessary for the inner journey and we share the presence of the God who is in our midst and in our hearts. That sharing takes place in silence and in stillness. Now consider these words of Jesus again:

He who sent me is present with me, and has not left me alone. . . . If you dwell within the revelation I have brought, you are indeed my disciples; you shall know the truth, and

110

the truth will set you free. . . . If then the Son sets you free, you will indeed be free.[2]

2. John 8:29, 31–2, 36

The Accuracy of Sacrifice

In a previous incarnation – that is, before I became a monk – I served in the Counter Intelligence Service and one of the jobs that I had to do was to locate radio stations operated by the enemy. And so we would tune in our receivers to them, but the enemy were very clever and if they were operating say on a frequency of ninety metres, at eighty-nine metres they would send out a jamming wave, a jamming signal, and at ninety-one they would send out another. So, in order to tune in exactly on their station you had to have an extremely fine tuning on your own radio. But we liked to think that we were just as clever as the enemy and so, when we found out the frequencies that they were broadcasting on, we took quartz crystals and then we would plug in the crystal to our receiver. Our receiver would then pick up their signal absolutely spot on, and none of the jamming devices interfered with it.

I was just thinking about this the other day when it struck me that the mantra is very like a quartz crystal. The enemy that we all face, our ego, is sending out all sorts of contrary signals around the wavelength of God, and what we have to do is to get on the 'God frequency' exactly, or as exactly as we can. As you all know from your own experience, the mantra is not magic. It is not an incantation, and learning to say your mantra means learning to follow a way of life in which *everything* in your life is attuned to God. And so, in a sense, everything in your life is attuned to the mantra.

The essence of the Christian message is that God is a present reality, and this is to say that God is a reality who is present to us. If you consider for a moment that 'God is present' you begin to understand that he is present in every moment of our life and is so because of the extravagant generosity of Jesus.

The Presence is communicated through Jesus. The call to each one of us is to respond to his presence and to live in it. To respond to his generosity we become present to him ourselves. That means our hearts are open to him at all times. The generosity of Jesus demands of us that we seek that Presence selflessly, not so that we will become wiser or holier, not so that we will possess God, but simply because it is right and fitting that we respond to his generous self-giving, his generous self-sacrifice by our own self-giving and our own self-sacrifice.

The challenge of meditation is that it does make each of us face the basic redemptive question. The basic question is, 'Do we seek God or do we seek ourselves?' Another way of phrasing that would be to say, 'Do we seek our destiny within our own confined limits, do we seek to define ourselves merely within our own resources, or do we seek our destiny beyond ourselves, in God?' That is what our meditation is about – seeking to burst the limits imposed on us by our own egoism. The tragedy of Faust, for example, was that he threw away his eternal destiny for the perishable, limited crown of mere worldly fulfilment. Faust is such a tragedy because he knew that that was what he had done. It is knowledge that underlies so much of the anxiety and fear of our society.

Now the challenge for us is not to reject the world nor to reject ourselves. The challenge is to learn to sacrifice. To sacrifice we offer something to God, and in the Jewish law it is the whole thing that was offered. It was called a holocaust. Nothing was kept back. Everything was given to God. That is what our meditation does to our life. The mantra, our meditation, enables us to lose ourselves entirely, to offer ourselves entirely, in our wholeness, to God. It helps us to become a holocaust in which everything we are is offered to God unconditionally. That is why we keep only the mantra sounding. When the time comes, we are prepared to surrender that too, because in our meditation we are entirely at his disposition. We exist only in his presence and we are in his presence because of his generosity. The wonderful thing about meditation is that in this self-sacrifice and loss of self, his Presence becomes our presence and his generosity becomes our generosity. As we persevere in meditation the loss of self becomes more and more complete, the sacrifice becomes more and more perfect and so the generosity is constantly increasing. That is why I stress to you so often the importance of saying your mantra from the beginning to the end of your time of meditation. No thought, no words, no imagination, no ideas. Remember the holocaust, the sacrifice. Now perhaps this is the greatest thing that we can do as conscious human beings – to offer our consciousness to God. In offering it we become fully conscious.

This is the experience of St Paul when he is speaking about the nearness of God:

> The peace of God, which is beyond our utmost understanding, will keep guard over your hearts and your thoughts, in Christ Jesus.[1]

What we have to learn is to seek that peace absolutely. Some people would think that it is unwise to speak of the absolute commitment that Jesus calls us to. Some people would think that even to hear about it is only for experts. But as far as I can understand it, the invitation of Jesus is given to each of us to take up our cross, to follow him to Calvary and to join him in his sacrifice and to go through with him, into the infinite love of the Father.

1. Phil. 4:7